Leadership Fit For The Future Of Work

ORLA KELLY PUBLISHING

Marianne Roux

978-1-915502-57-5
 The information in this book was compiled from transcribed interviews with leaders in their field who consented to the published, in addition to the author's viewpoint and expertise from over 30 years working in the area of leadership and their PhD thesis findings. Cover design by 2funkidesign. Published in Ireland by Orla Kelly Publishing.

Orla Kelly Publishing
27 Kilbrody,
Mount Oval,
Rochestown,
Cork,
Ireland.

About the Author

Marianne Roux has 30 years of global experience as an HR Executive, Future Work Strategist and Professor of Leadership. She holds a master's degree in HR and Organisational Psychology and has a PhD in Leadership in the Future of Work. She runs Roux Consulting, a global niche consulting firm based in Dublin, Ireland and regularly teaches at Business Schools worldwide.

She has worked for PWC, Accenture, Deloitte and Mercer and has held two HR Director roles in two countries, Woolworths Food South Africa and Cricket Australia.

Her experience spans several industries, including Retail, FMCG, Mining, Oil and Gas, Public Sector, Utilities, Infrastructure, Media, Financial services, Telecommunications, Sport, NFP, Health and Pharmaceutical and Tech start-ups.

Her work focuses mainly on the Future of Work Strategy, Leadership Development, Organisation Redesign and HR transformation.

She is a published author of Adaptive HR and a Personal Agility reflection journal: Knowing Your Superpowers is the Key to Your Success in a Changing World, and she is featured in Maturing Leadership: How Adult Development Impact Leadership.

Marianne works pro-bono on developing women and alleviating poverty and trauma. She has served on the Boards of Hagar Australia, Hagar International, YGAP and the Edmund Rice Foundation.

She was chosen as one of 52 inspirational women at work in South Africa in 2004 and one of 20 Female Entrepreneurs by Management Today in 2011 in Australia. In 2015, she won the Excellence in NFP Consulting award from the Worldwide Who's Who.

Chapters

CHAPTER 1

Introduction

Many people think leadership is easy and fun. However, the more responsibility you assume, the more uncertainty you will be expected to manage. Uncertainty is not the enemy but is the opportunity. The leader's responsibility is to bring clarity in the midst of paradox and ambiguity.

Dennis Hooper

Many leaders are caught in the transition between the practices and principles that defined the industrial era and the new reality of the twenty-first century.

Attempts to achieve collaboration, empowerment, and diversity in organizations fail because the beliefs and thought processes of leaders as well as employees are stuck in an old paradigm that values control, stability, and homogeneity.

The difficult transition between the old and the new partly explains the current crisis in organizational leadership.

Daft

There are about 70,000 books on leadership. Why another one? Because we are still looking for the answers. Over the thirty years I have spent as a leadership and leadership development researcher and practitioner, I have always been baffled by the amount of money (about $366 billion per annum) spent on leadership development and the corresponding lacklustre impact it achieves. The development does not stick, behaviours do not change, and leadership quality does not improve.

Many argue that our workplaces are even more toxic than ever, and leaders are not coping well with the complexity and ambiguity they must contend with. Dan Pontefract recently quotes results from the DDI 2023 Global Leadership Forecast that found an alarming decline in high-quality leaders globally (a 17% drop from last year). The major contributor to this is the deterioration of trust and high levels of burnout.

I spent the last six years completing a PhD study to make sense of these challenges. I reviewed the literature and leadership development literature. I interviewed twenty-two leadership development experts and practitioners to understand what works and does not work in leadership and leadership development theory and practice. I also wanted to understand it in the context of the 'future of work' – with its complexity and ambiguity.

The findings were stark – we are using outdated and fixed leadership models. We are still wedded to competencies and traits, the individual hero leader and easy, quick fixes. We are still developing leaders using short, programmatic and one-dimensional approaches. We are still not evaluating impact and application or focusing on embedding new mindsets and practices. We love edutainment and fun days at wonderful venues with good food and parties. We are not even using solid evidence-based theory and practice. Pfeffer (2016) criticises the plethora of content and practices of leadership and leadership development that are not validated and have not improved trust and engagement.

Most programs comprise ideas leading to conceptual overload and low retention. Pick up any article or book on leadership, and you will see a rehash and renaming of the same concepts in different "fads". Most approaches do not tackle the complexity of leadership and leadership development and how humans learn and change, nor does it reflect how the world of work has changed – the agility, collaboration and human-centric nature of leadership that is required now.

After analysing the literature and interviews, I developed an updated and integrated model of leadership and a contextual framework for leadership development fit for complex and uncertain environments. I tested the model and frameworks in real-life, complex, large-scale leadership development programs and analysed the lessons learnt. The models are underpinned by the key finding that context affects leadership, and leadership affects context. Human behaviour change theories and development's iterative and ongoing nature also underpin it.

I conducted further interviews with organisations and leaders applying these frameworks in their development programs and leadership practices for this book. Let me start with two conversations I had for this book with leaders I admire and have worked with to help you understand what it looks like.

Giam Swiegers, Chairman Aurecon & Chairman Attvest Finance. Former Global CEO of Aurecon and CEO of Deloitte Australia. Founding member, Male Champions for Change

"It is a complicated time in which to lead. All my experience is in Professional Services or organisations related to Professional Services. These organisations are all about the people. The mood of the people plays a significant role in the actual product. If you are running a manufacturing plant, someone might buy a chair from you and my experience of the chair is not affected by the mood of the employees that made the chair. In Professional Services, consumption and production take place at the same time. So, the only way to ensure the clients get high quality is to have talented people committed to solving the client's problem. So, for me it was always about how people can give that little bit extra in applying their minds.

One controversy I had in Deloitte and Aurecon, both turnaround situations, is that the traditional mantra in Professional Services is that it is all about the client. The client comes first. I turned that around and was clear in my business model that our people were the apex of our business model. We had to do what was good for our people because only then would they do what was good for the client. When I walked into Deloitte Australia, we had unhappy people. We were screaming all the time, "it is all about clients, it is all about clients", but we sent unhappy people out to clients So, I wanted to make people happy about the firm and proud to wear the jumper.

Focusing on the people is all about leadership and the environment they create. The quote I always use when I talk about this topic is: "leadership is not about taking people where they want to go; it is about taking people where they ought to go: And I add, "if you can make the destination where they ought to go attractive enough so that they want to go there, then the battle is won".

People are complex because every individual is different it is hard to drive innovation with people that are all different. But it is impossible to drive innovation without people. Create a culture where people of diversity can flourish and bring their best ideas. Warren Bennis says: "There are two ways to be creative: once can sing and dance, or once can create the environment in which singers and dancers can flourish". Every time I do a leadership presentation, I put this up and say: "I don't mind if you cannot sing and dance, but if you cannot create an environment where diverse people and creatives can flourish, you are out of here".

As you know, Deloitte and Aurecon were voted as the most innovative companies in Australia– you must find a goal that excites all the people while allowing them a certain amount of freedom to be themselves. You cannot take conventional thinkers and ask them to find unconventional new solutions, so a part is recruiting people from the outside, and another part is discovering those innovative people already in the organisation suppressed by conventional leaders.

You must have layers and layers of leaders – not a single charismatic leader. It is about leaders who create teams of leaders that all lead considering the organisation's overall goals, their service offering's goals and the context in which they lead. For example, every city in Australia is different. When I was with Aurecon, we operated in 28 countries that are all different – you cannot manage it from the centre.

I try to look back at my week or month, and I ask myself whether I spent over 50% with my people. That could be talking to people, listening to their issues, presenting plans, recruiting people, convincing people to stay, convincing people to join, debating who should be promoted or identifying high-potential talent. I want to ensure I am reading the mood, knowing what bothers them, and removing the filters and barriers for them.

I used voicemails in Deloitte and emails to all staff emails at Aurecon, and that style has a lot of quirkiness. The voicemails were wonderful because they would come from the heart and were serious and playful. Then technology (mobile phones) changed everything, and at Aurecon, having people in 28 countries, it was even harder to connect with everyone. So, I made sure every time I travelled between offices, and I would write an email to all our people starting with "I am on a plane". I would explain to them where I was and where I was going. I wrote about what I am proud of, what worked well and what I was concerned about. This helped the office I was going to understand what I valued and what was on my mind. So often, I would go up in the lift, and someone would say. "That one email really resonated with me". If you don't like it, you can delete it, but if you were interested in what was happening in the organisation, this could connect you. I am convinced more than half of people read it, and even if only a third of people read it, I would still do it. I believe in keeping people informed, but not with edited corporate BS, real messages from my heart, written by me. If your emails do not sound like the way you speak, people will not trust them."

Brid Horan – Chancellor Dublin City University, Independent Chair and Non-Executive Director, Founding member 30% Club Ireland

The first thing Brid says when I interview her is, "I don't think of myself as a leader", which sums up the beautiful humility she shows up with when you meet her. Yet she has had an outsized impact as a leader in Ireland – both a business leader and a diversity champion. I ask her what drives her. She says:

"I want to change things if they are not right. When I started as a trainee actuary, I realised I was not being paid the same as my male counterparts. When I questioned this, I was told I was on the female pay scale, to which I replied that it was unfair practice. I was then told I could move to the same pay if I passed my exam, to which I then asked whether this would be back paid. So, I decided to put a motion to the union for fair and equal pay, which was accepted – this is how I got involved in the union movement. I stood for the Union Committee and became involved in more women's issues. The need for fairness drove me.

As I took some time out as a young mother and re-entered my career, I continued working on issues of equity and fairness. I was one of the founding members of the 30% club in Ireland (a global campaign supported by Board Chairs and CEOs of medium and large organisations to achieve better gender balance at leadership levels). I got involved in Industry Associations and Board Director roles. All these experiences helped me to continue to step up to make a bigger difference. The diversity of roles and experiences provides a wonderful set of different experiences to draw on.

Often, I was terrified, but I was more fearful of things NOT changing, so I went ahead anyway. What got me through was a sense of curiosity, a dash of courage and the need to make connections. I accept that I cannot know everything or what is coming, and I do as well as I can by taking one step and gaining momentum. You can only gather so much evidence, then you must back your and others' judgments. I do not want perfect to be the enemy of better. I had to learn the hard way when I could not get momentum on a critical project that you HAVE to do something different to get a different outcome. But you must stay focused on your values to guide you."

How this book is structured

In the first two chapters, I introduce you to the topic, define what I mean by the term "Future of Work" and help you put the challenges leaders face into context. In Chapter 3, I explain why our current leadership models and leadership development approaches are inadequate in helping leaders thrive in the complexity of the future of work context.

Chapter 4 covers the findings from my research about effective leadership in the future of work context and the six mindsets and practices found to help leaders thrive. Chapter 5 describes the research findings on six contextual dimensions that need to be considered when designing and delivering leadership development to be impactful in the future of work context.

The next part of the book then takes the evidence and frameworks provided and breaks them down into mindsets, practices, reflections and tools to help organisations and individuals get their arms around their development. In chapters 6 to 11, I provide a detailed description, real leadership examples, tools, and learning resources for each of the six leadership mindsets and practices.

The final chapter brings all the research and practices together. I reflect on the paradoxical nature of leadership and how these leaders and organisations are leaning into this challenge.

A final thought before you start.

Leadership is a journey, not a destination. The journey is both an inner and an outer journey. It is full of ups and downs. There is no endpoint. It is a lifelong commitment and choice. You are always learning and evolving. Every context and disruption you lead needs careful consideration.

As you start on this journey - assess your gaps and set your goals (only a few at a time) – but also develop your own immunity maps to understand where you need to be more aware of competing commitments. Be intentional about your focus, and you're learning. Do not just re-use the same knowledge, mindsets, and habits to solve new and different challenges.

Prioritise the mindsets and skills you want to work in for the first 12 months. Develop them in a focused way by using sprints. But remember, this is not a solo journey. Journey with other leaders – support, challenge, teach and inspire each other.

Work through your discomfort. You will go through a cycle of behavioural change that looks and feels something like the picture in Figure 1. You might feel *that is not me they are talking about*, then as you learn, you might get a niggling feeling it might be a development area, but you do not know how to develop it. That is when you must be curious and disciplined and spend the time learning and practising.

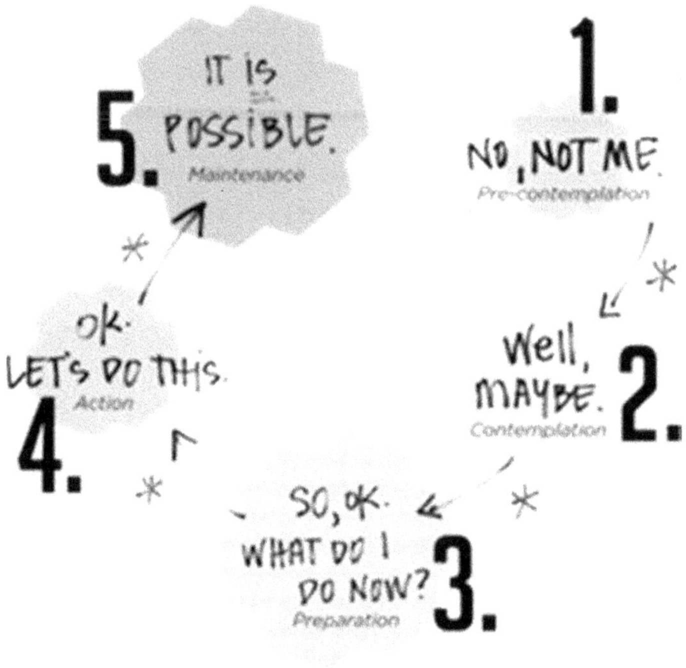
1.
NO, NOT ME.
Pre-contemplation
Well, MAYBE.
2.
Contemplation
SO, OK. WHAT DO I DO NOW?
3.
Preparation
OK. LET'S DO THIS.
4.
Action
IT IS POSSIBLE.
5.
Maintenance

Figure 1: Behaviour change cycle

Source: http://persuasive.cut.ac.cy/2016/06/18/designing-for-different-stages-in-behaviour-change/

You need to practice a lot. Repeat your new mindsets and practices until they become your new automatic behaviours. Do not underestimate the number of repetitions and practice you need to continue with (see Figure 2).

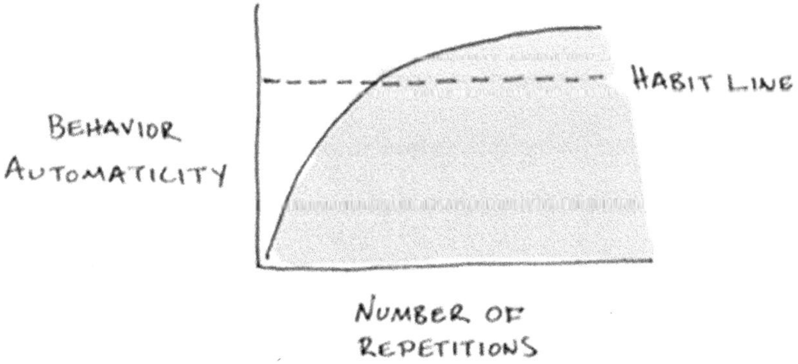
HABIT LINE
BEHAVIOR
AUTOMATICITY
NUMBER OF
REPETITIONS

Figure 2: Behaviour automaticity and repetition

Source: James Clear

Deliberate practice works because it increases myelin (a layer of fatty tissue that grows around neurons and acts as an insulator that allows the cells to fire faster and cleaner). By focusing your attention, you are forcing the specific circuit to fire again and again in isolation. This triggers cells called oligodendrocytes to begin wrapping layers of myelin around neurons in the circuits – cementing the skill or behaviour. So, DO leadership, learn, connect, and achieve – repeat and get a little better daily.

CHAPTER 2

The Future Of Work Context

The future of work describes changes in how work will get done over the next decade, influenced by technological, generational and social shifts.

Gartner

The future of work refers to changes that technology (automation, AI, robotics) along with new employment models (freelancers, gig workers and crowds) will bring about in how we work, who we work with, and the skills and capabilities we need to work.

Schwartz and Riss

The disruptive influence of technology and automation on societies, economies, and organizations and the rise of the knowledge economy is widely documented. What is less well-known is how these trends affect the human work experience, adult intellect, and adult development.

Ackerman and Kanfer

The current context leaders lead in is the 'future of work' or some call it the "now of work". It is an idea that is not well understood and agreed.

The 'future of work' has been around since 2014, but the pandemic has accelerated the pace of it. Gartner shows in Figure 3 how cumulative seismic shifts have changed how we work, where we work and how we feel about work. The hybrid revolution collides with the acceleration of Artificial Intelligence (AI), automation, and a strong focus on Environment, Social and Governance (ESG) matters, creating the perfect storm. It is also leading to calls for a more human approach.

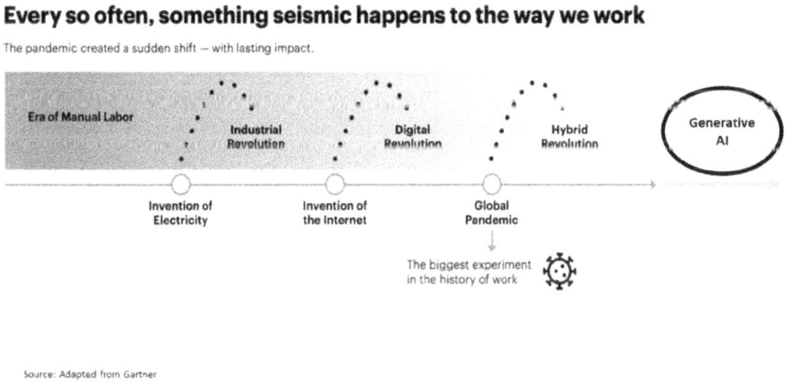
Every so often, something seismic happens to the way we work
The pandemic created a sudden shift – with lasting impact.
Era of Manual Labor
Industrial Revolution
Digital Revolution
Hybrid Revolution
Generative AI
Invention of Electricity
Invention of the Internet
Global Pandemic
The biggest experiment in the history of work
Source: Adapted from Gartner

Figure 3: Seismic change from the pandemic

Source: Adapted from Cambon, A. & Walker, G. (2021)

There is now a further seismic shift in the form of Generative Artificial Intelligence (AI). Early reports from Goldman Sachs already say 300 million jobs will be affected by generative AI across major economies. But it is estimated that productivity gains could boost global GDP by 7%. A real moral dilemma if ever I saw one! (Strauss, 2023). How do you commit to responsible and ethical AI and reskilling people to a sustainable future? How do we use the best of what humans are capable of?

Qualtrics defines the future of work in 2023 as making business more human and establishing deeper, more meaningful connections through our work. They ascribe these renewed focuses because of COVID-19 impacts on remote work and virtual meetings, exponential growth in e-commerce and the acceleration of automation and AI adoption. The subsequent great resignation and quiet quitting sent shockwaves through organisations and further geopolitical and personal cost of living challenges created further instability for everyone.

I use the term 'future of work' as an umbrella term to capture all complexity, contradictions, and tensions associated with Industry 4.0 and 5.0, hybrid work, skills-based talent approaches, focus on wellbeing, inclusion, social and environmental justice (ESG), and other unexpected challenges like COVID-19, wars, and inflation. Leaders are dancing on a shifting carpet all the time. Let's unpack the concepts I include in my definition, starting with Industries 4.0 and 5.0, as shown in Figure 4 below.

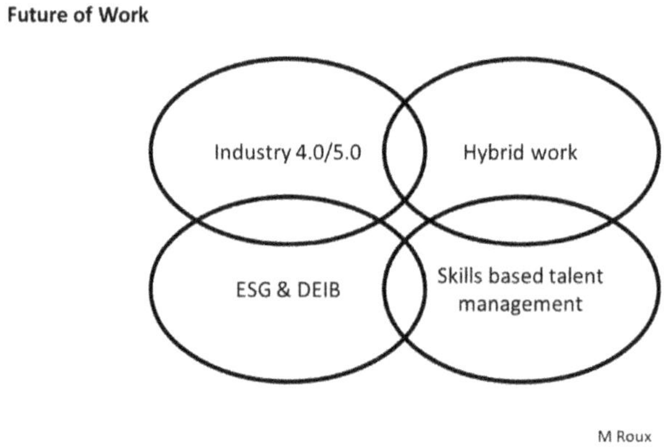
Future of Work
Industry 4.0/5.0
Hybrid work
ESG & DEIB
Skills based talent management
M Roux

Figure 4: Future of work

Let's unpack each of these more. Robleck, Meskp and Krapez (2016) write that the phenomenon of **Industry 4.0** was first mentioned in Germany as a proposal for developing a new economic policy based on a high-tech strategy. It is marked by full automation, intelligent production, and digitisation of processes, and advanced technologies like artificial intelligence, big data, and connectivity. This has led to increased competition, changes to consumer behaviour and obsolete and new mindsets, jobs, and skills in organisations. Although believed to have kicked off around 2014, a lot of organisations were slow out of the starting block, and Industry 4.0 implementations stalled during the pandemic, leaders are desperately trying to catch up while managing costs in a recessionary environment.

Whilst many companies are still getting their heads around 4.0, 5.0 is being discussed more. The term **Industry 5.0** was first used in 2017 when Japan shared its vision of an idea called Society 5.0 at the CeBIT fair in Germany. Industry 5.0 focuses on bringing the human, social, and environmental dimensions back into the equation of technological advances. As 2022 research by Boyden indicates, "Industry 5.0 marks the end of an era in which organisations focused primarily on unlocking the potential of technologies. The emphasis is now on human potential". Boyden Executive Survey, (2022) (https:// www.boyden.com/media/strengthening-the-human-centric-core-of-industry-50-27765859/index.html)

Industry 5.0 "provides a vision of industry that aims beyond efficiency and productivity as the sole goals and reinforces the role and the contribution of industry to society." and "It places the wellbeing of the worker at the centre of the production process and uses new technologies to provide prosperity beyond jobs and growth while respecting the production limits of the planet." It complements the Industry 4.0 approach by "specifically putting research and innovation at the service of the transition to a *sustainable, human-centric* and *resilient European industry*". It calls for a human-centric strategy focused on talent (skills), diversity and empowerment. It is an agile, resilient, and sustainable approach to business and organisations. (Kraaijenbrink, 2022).

The employee landscape will continue to change profoundly. McKinsey estimates that over 50% of current work activities are technically automatable and that 400-800 million individuals could be displaced and need to find new jobs by 2030. Fortunately, although new technology may displace certain types of jobs, history has shown us that technology has created more jobs than it has taken. The challenge is the transition paths for workers to have access to **skills** required for new jobs. We face the opportunity to make work more human by expanding humans' role on teams with machines and focusing on creativity and context. (Schwartz & Riss, 2021). But we can only do so I leaders are committed to and know how to do this.

We are reaching the "end of jobs" (Jesuthasan and Boudreau, 2022). Skills are the currency of the future. Many organisations are now deconstructing jobs, mapping skills (current and future), upskilling and reskilling at scale and deploying talent through flexible project work and talent marketplaces. With skills only 2–5-year life, learning and skilling will be a critical focus for organisations.

The pandemic changed how we work and feel about work forever in all these challenges. **Hybrid and remote** work at scale is a new phenomenon post-pandemic. The challenge for leaders is maintaining belonging, connection and culture in this new way of working. Leaders must be more intentional about inclusivity, collaboration, meetings, and communication. At the same time, they must design focused and collaborative work so that high levels of productivity and performance are maintained without burning out employees. Empathy and compassion will become critical leadership mindsets and practices.

Finally, every leader must understand **ESG**. It has become an executive-level business issue, given strong and rising interest from investors, consumers, and regulators. ESG has also catapulted to the top for talent as they choose who they work for. They ask themselves: what is the ESG strategy, can I have a social impact in my role? What is the organisation's purpose, and does it align with mine? Do they care about my life and my well-being? Is this an inclusive organisation, is there pay equity? Can I bring my whole self to work here?

The 'future of work' perspective is critical for successful leadership. What is not clear is whether our approaches to leadership and leadership development have evolved to enable leaders to thrive in this context. Amy Cohen (2023) writes that paradoxes are endemic in this complex environment where mega issues are converging and gaining momentum. Leaders need to get the balance right on multiple fronts. An example is the increasing pressure on leaders to show they care about people AND the increasing pressure on leaders to sustain performance and deliver results.

Too often, leaders polarise themselves or are stuck in a preference. A paradoxical environment calls for a paradoxical leader – in both the environment AND in themselves. It is not about being perfect but embracing the AND, not going for the OR. Embracing this thinking is tricky because it goes against how our brains work – the brain prefers simplicity, quick solutions and efficient decision-making. The future of work context is making this increasingly challenging, and we have to adapt.

Let's see how two brave organisations have leaned into this idea to ensure they and their people thrive in a complex future.

NASA has a Future of Work Framework developed by the Chief Human Capital Officer to understand the disruptors driving the future of work and implications for NASA so it can evolve talent strategies aligned with the new work, workforce, and workplace of tomorrow. Their framework is shown in Figure 5.

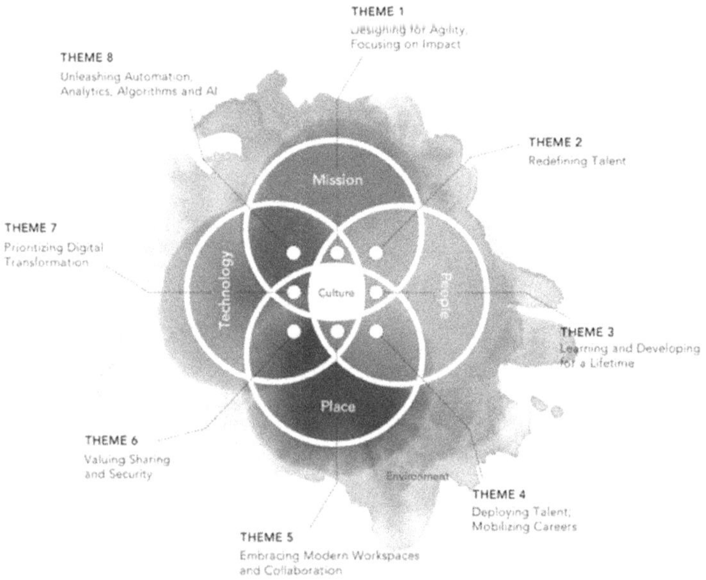
THEME 1
Designing for Agility, Focusing on Impact
THEME 2
Redefining Talent
THEME 3
Learning and Developing for a Lifetime
THEME 4
Deploying Talent; Mobilizing Careers
THEME 5
Embracing Modern Workspaces and Collaboration
THEME 6
Valuing Sharing and Security
THEME 7
Prioritizing Digital Transformation
THEME 8
Unleashing Automation, Analytics, Algorithms and AI
Mission
People
Place
Technology
Culture
Environment

Figure 5: NASA Future of Work framework

The eight themes emerged from research findings categorized into four major overlapping meta forces: mission, people, place, and technology. Themes range from rethinking the roles of organizations and individuals, to embracing the role technology increasingly augments and enable the workforce. (Skytland,2018)

Unilever developed a clear response to the Future of Work which they launched in 2016 – it was an overarching plan to prepare the workforce for a digitalised and highly automated era, It focused on accelerating the speed of change within Unilever, reskilling staff through a culture of lifelong learning and adopting flexible work practices. In 2020 the strategy was reviewed to further rapid changes in the FMCG industry (Kerr et al, 2020). The plan is shown in Figure 6.

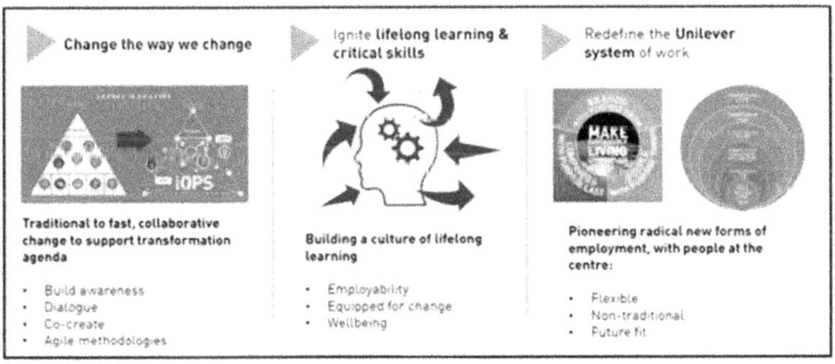
Change the way we change
Ignite lifelong learning & critical skills
Redefine the Unilever system of work
IOPS
MAKE LIVING
Traditional to fast, collaborative change to support transformation agenda
Build awareness
Dialogue
Co-create
Agile methodologies
Building a culture of lifelong learning
Employability
Equipped for change
Wellbeing
Pioneering radical new forms of employment, with people at the centre:
Flexible
Non-traditional
Future fit

Source: Company Data.

Figure 6: Unilever Future of Work plan

The plan has three focuses: 1) Change the way we change; 2) Ignite lifelong learning and critical skills and 3) Redefine the Unilever system of work.

Do you have a clear and shared view and strategy of the Future of Work in your organisation?

CHAPTER 3

Current Leadership And Leadership Development Approaches Are Not Delivering The Needed Impact

The need for re-imaging leadership becomes even more critical if viewed against the backdrop of the deepening, widening crisis around leadership worldwide. Globally people increasingly are angry at, frustrated with, skeptical of, alienated from, disillusioned with, mistrusting of, loathing of, raging, and revolting against current leaders and leadership, and the organisations and institutions they represent. The imperative is to grow re-imagined future-fit leadership, able to find and realise desired futures.

Veldsman

The story of the last 50 years of leadership development has been the story of the individual. It began with discoveries about "what" made a good leader and was followed by the development of practices that helped a generation of individuals move closer to that ideal. The workplace context rewarded individuals who could think through a situation analytically and then direct others to carry out well-thought-through procedures. The complexity of the new environment increasingly presents what Ronald Heifetz calls "adaptive challenges" in which it is not possible for any one individual to know the solution or even define the problem.

Petrie

We Are Not Developing Leaders Fit For The Future Of Work

Ignoring how the accelerating rate and magnitude of change reframes the future of work may contribute to leadership and leadership development (LD) that equips leaders to operate in a context that no longer exists. This myopic approach fails to deliver the impacts for organisations to thrive in a complex future. DeRue and Myers (2014) argue that, even though organisations are increasing their investments in leadership development, there is an emerging consensus that the supply of leadership talent is not enough to meet the leadership needs of modern organisations.

This research is corroborated by Kegan (1982), Cook-Greuter (2004) and Dawson (2015) that all found that leaders are "in over their heads." Cook-Greuter (2004) found that of 4,510 adults only half could work in later stage action logics (meaning making capabilities) compatible with the level of complexity leaders face in the changing context they work in (achiever, individualist, strategist, and unionist). Dawson (2015) similarly found that, of 512 leaders assessed for cognitive complexity, more than half could not operationalise systemic levels of thinking required in most managerial jobs. The results are shown in Figure 7.

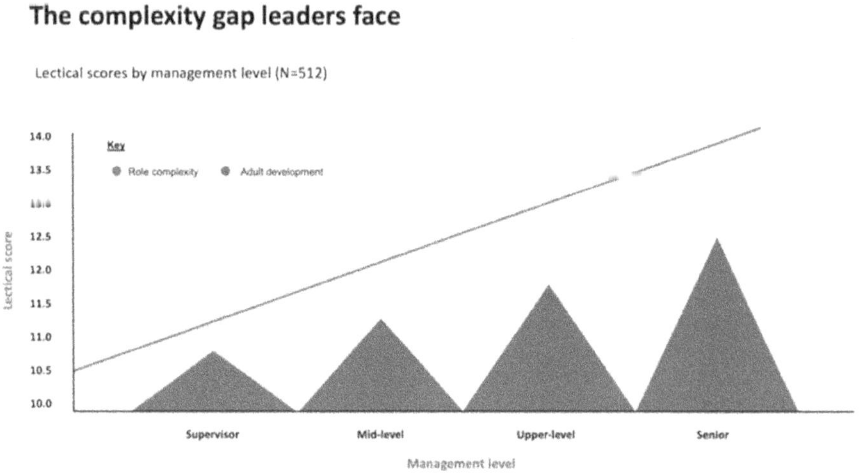
The complexity gap leaders face
Lectical scores by management level (N=512)
Key
Role complexity
Adult development
14.0
13.5
12.5
12.0
11.5
11.0
10.5
10.0
Lectical score
Supervisor
Mid-level
Upper-level
Senior
Management level

Figure 7: Lectica research on lectical levels across levels of leadership

We Do Not Understand Or Agree What Leadership Means

Leadership is probably the most written about social phenomenon of all time. The sheer number of definitions for the term leadership (about 60 taxonomies and theories) is evidence of this problem. There is no meta curriculum or agreed evidence-based frame for leadership in the new world of work. In fact, there seems to be conceptual redundancy – the same thing is being renamed and presented as new and different.

People also like easy and quick fixes. Pick up any of the popular books on leadership today, and you will still find a list of traits and competencies thought to be central to effective leadership. These viewpoints do not acknowledge the inherent complexity of human behaviour and the context within which this behaviour occurs.

Van Seters and Field (1990) describe leadership as "one of the most complex and multifaceted phenomena to which organisational and psychological research has been applied" (p. 43). Leadership is embedded in context and is socially constructed. Leading in complex and disruptive times needs complex leadership. Zhu, Song, Zhu, and Johnson (2019) conducted a bibliometric analysis of leadership articles between 1990-2017 to portray the landscape and trajectory of leadership research over time via co-citation and co-occurrence analyses. Only 15 studies addressed leadership in context.

We Do Not Understand Or Agree On Effective Leadership Development (LD)

In terms of how the future of work context impacts LD, Vince, and Pedler (2018) agree that LD is falling behind societal trends and falls short of the responsibility to prepare leaders for complex environments. Vogel, Reichard, Batistic and Cerne (2020) find that LD remains fragmented and needs a comprehensive, holistic review.

Several disparate leadership development (LD) approaches exist with no clearly agreed curriculum or guideline on the best way to develop leadership. As with leadership definitions, scholars, and practitioners prefer to focus on standardized, predictable, and observable approaches rather than the more difficult, nebulous factors of mindset, ethics, and adult development – the challenging vertical development required in complex contexts. Typical programs teach leadership theory, ideas, and principles; they promote leadership literacy but do not increase leadership competence.

This is because earlier attempts at guidelines for LD were functionalist and individual-focused. Functionalist approaches focus on the development of individual leaders' repertoires of techniques and tools to increase their effectiveness. Mabey's (2013) analysis of the literature on

LD in organisations found that a functionalist perspective dominates, with 82% of the studies showing a pre-occupation "with enhancing the qualities of individual leaders, as if they are personally capable of turning organizations around" (p. 6). Professional LD that overly emphasizes pre-defined skills or competencies disregards and fails to appreciate the ontological dimension of leaders' professional learning ("learning in becoming" process) and leadership practice ("doing as" process) to be professional leaders (Dall 'Alba, 2009). Trait theory fails to consider situations such that different situations may require different behaviours from leaders, such as when dealing with tame, wicked, and critical problems (Grint, 2008). It is the modern version of the "great man" or "hero" leadership theories.

Constructivist approaches regard LD as more of an identity transition and a social interaction. The frame of constructivist approaches is a better fit for the future of work. This is because knowledge and competencies are becoming more transient due to the rapidity of change in the future of work. Constructivist approaches are influenced by adult development theory – it assumes people constantly make sense of themselves and their experiences, therefore continuously growing and changing as they progress to higher levels of complexity.

My research reveals that most leadership and leadership development models and practices are detached from context, and nuances of context are the most important factor to consider when developing leaders. Most programs do not leverage an understanding of human behaviour. Leadership development consultants often over-pack their programs with so many concepts, models, frameworks, and "insights "that they create overwhelm, and under-application. Fundamental behavioural change is rare, and participants usually regress to old patterns within weeks.

Noah Rabinowitz (2023) writes:

"For many years I've been observing the claims made by the $350B+ leadership development and learning industry. Many of them promise giant leaps in performance, rapid skill mastery, quick differentiating advantages, and easy fixes to underlying performance issues. These elusive promises are enabled by an engine of fragmented data elements that they use to support self-declared and cyclical trends and predictions.

A sampling of these unrealistic claims include:

Become a Better Leader Faster with These 5 Moves {article} Become a Better Leader Today!! {leadership program}

Improvement takes significant discipline and hard work in most fields (music, art, science, medicine, the trades, engineering, military, sport). It's slow, non-linear, and tedious and requires persistence and resilience. Steady consistent gains, accrued in small amounts over time, generally provide a path towards excellence. Easy shortcuts or workarounds don't actually exist – even when pitched or promised to us by experts.

Measuring LD impact is rare. Russon and Reinelt (2004) evaluated the results of 55 LD programs and found that most focused on individual outcomes, few had an explicit program theory, and almost none had the resources to conduct longitudinal evaluations. Leadership researchers and practitioners have not focused enough on the impact, value, and relevance of their interventions or on their own accreditation and knowledge renewal. LD designers continue to evaluate LD using perceptions of success and reaction criteria at the end of their programmatic interventions and very few use results criteria throughout the learning journey to adapt the programs for more impact."

CHAPTER 4

A New Way Of Thinking About Leadership

A great leader in the new world of work is someone who can build teams, understand the implications of technology on business, adapt to the speed at which business is happening, operate at a high level and a low level simultaneously and build trust across the organisation to get things done.

Schwartz and Riss

The signs point to a future of work that is authentically human, in all its complexity. To succeed in that, the leaders of tomorrow must be equally open and complex—with all the adaptability, empathy and inclusivity that entails.

Stephen Bailey

Mature leaders handle complexity well because they themselves are more complex – in their thinking, identities, emotional management, behavioural repertoire, and social competence. They don't oversimplify their role or their personality.

Mature leaders have changed and developed over time, and they are aware that there has been an evolution.

Ted Billies

Leadership is complex because of the discontinuous and disruptive change of the context leaders lead in. Ted Billies (2015) writes that complexity means more than just "very complicated". It involves interrelatedness and unpredictability, as in complex systems

... it's the grey between the black and white, the nuances beneath opposing positions. In this context, businesses and organizations are facing frequent – even continuous – disruptive change and constraints to growth. On an individual level, such complexity can feel like information overload, chaos, ambiguity – a recipe for confusion and anxiety. This makes it particularly challenging for leaders responsible for making high-stake decisions that provide clarity amidst the confusion.

And given the increasing interdependence of our economic, political, and social systems, the role of business leaders has shifted from action primarily aimed inward and down on their business to action upward and out – into the community, society and the international economic and political arenas. Whether they recognize it or not, leaders of large, geographically dispersed organizations are integral to a global network of forces and decisions that impact the whole system.

So, how do we start to make sense of leadership fit for this context? We must look back to look forward first. Yammarino (2013) describes the history of leadership in three stages: the past (antiquity to 1900), the present (1900-2012) and the future (2012-2025). The past focused on renowned and prominent leaders and some social reformers but with no systematic scholarly research to back this up. The year 1900 marks the start of scholarly research into leadership. Before 1970, most leadership research focused on the leader as a person, the group they led and the effectiveness of that group, and leadership styles became popular. In the 1970s, the focus shifted to multiple leader-follower relationships and dyads. In the 1980s, 1990s and 2000s, another set of ideas emerged that focused more on collectivist leadership.

Leadership has evolved over several eras, under the evolving Industrial Revolutions (IRs). In the first IR, charismatic leadership was related to how leaders act and mobilize an organization through actions and personal features. In Leadership 1.0, the natural born leader was a widespread notion – the great man theory.

The second IR was strongly shaped by scientific management, in which leaders assume a top-down style and could be characterized as directive leadership. Leadership 2.0 was the era of scientific management. For the third IR, leadership was characterized by relational leadership, considering the theories of transformational leadership to stimulate the autonomy of followers for new ideas, collaboration among them.

Leadership 3.0 came about in the late 1970s, when various studies and discussions on transformational leadership called for a more engaged leadership where the leader builds a meaningful relationship with the follower. The fourth IR requires both existing features and new required features from leadership. It needs more than a transformational leadership. It also needs a more specific focus on learning and innovation. Writers like Gloor (2017) and Kelly (2019) describe Leadership as adaptive, emergent, connected, responsive, and collaborative – Leadership 4.0.

Part of the challenge we face in making sense of where we are, is that many paradigms either exclude each other rather than integrate; and ideas were added to each other, creating a proliferation of constructs and construct redundancy. Most challenging, though, is the continued use of outdated theories. All theories should be scrutinized and assessed in their relevance to the organisation's and the future of work contexts. New theories and practices like complexity and systems leadership, crisis leadership, the developmental approach to leadership, digital leadership, virtual and hybrid leadership, and human leadership should be tested. With what we learn, we need to work towards a broad framework for the future of work context.

In my research, emerging vantage points are that leadership is a complex phenomenon and needs complex, shared and human leadership. In the context of the future of work and ongoing disruption, leaders need to work across boundaries to bring together disparate and diverse sets of people, processes, and technologies and reconfigure them in real time to increase the likelihood of organization survival – being responsive, resilient, and agile. Here is a depiction of how leadership has evolved in Table 1.

Leadership is evolving

Leadership 1.0	Leadership 2.0 and 3.0	Leadership 4.0
Hero leadership	Visionary	SHARED
Trait theory	Charismatic	**Human**
Command and control	Transformational	Integrative
Competencies	Behavioral	Holistic, deep
Job security	Horizontal	Eco systemic
Hierarchy	Competencies	Lifelong journey
Narrow tasks and roles	Empowerment	Complex social context
Socialized	Culture	Neuroplasticity
For the elite few	Socialized	Horizontal and vertical
	Situational	Agile and adaptive
		Digital technology
		Virtual and flexible
		Self-authoring
		Purposeful and values driven

M Roux

Table 1: How leadership has evolved

Reflect on the evolution of leadership. What is your current vantage point? Has it evolved to reflect the complexity of Industries 4 and 5.0?

So, what does leadership look like almost in terms of mindsets, practices, and competencies in Industry 4.0 and 5.0? In my research, I found there are six critical elements leaders must collectively develop over time to lead effectively of work. These include Contextual Intelligence, Personal Agility and Curiosity, Ethical and Moral Maturity, Identity, Collaborative Behaviours and Future Fit Competencies as shown in Figure 8.

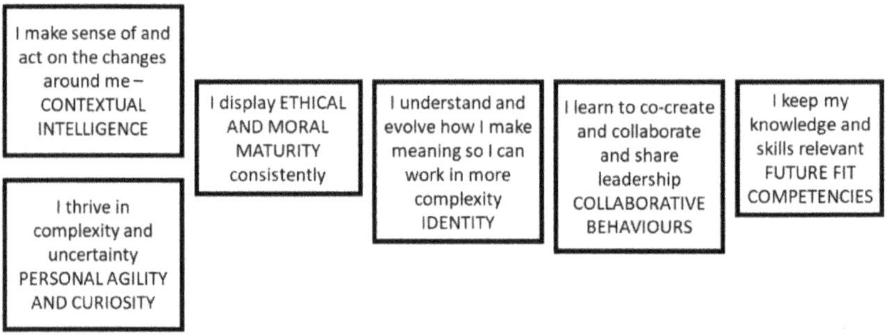
I make sense of and act on the changes around me – CONTEXTUAL INTELLIGENCE
I thrive in complexity and uncertainty PERSONAL AGILITY AND CURIOSITY
I display ETHICAL AND MORAL MATURITY consistently
I understand and evolve how I make meaning so I can work in more complexity IDENTITY
I learn to co-create and collaborate and share leadership COLLABORATIVE BEHAVIOURS
I keep my knowledge and skills relevant FUTURE FIT COMPETENCIES

Figure 8: Leadership fit for the future of work

Let's have a closer look at each of these:

Contextual intelligence – because of the complexity and uncertainty of today's leadership context, leaders need contextual intelligence –

the awareness of the continually changing context and the ability to behave in a contextually intelligent manner using hindsight, insight, and foresight.

Personal agility and curiosity – The mindsets and practices of Personal Agility and Curiosity are Growth Mindset, Self-Awareness, Emotional Agility, Grit, and Focus. You can build these by re-aligning your mindsets, actions, emotions, and thoughts to your values and become more conscious of your behaviour.

Ethical and moral maturity – Ethical and moral maturity is characterised by depth and consistency of moral judgements and advanced abilities to navigate ethical dilemmas.

Identity – "the sub-component of one's identity that relates to being a leader or how one thinks of oneself as a leader" (Day & Harrison, 2007, p. 365). Identity is important in leadership as it grounds you in understanding who you are and helps define who you want to be.

Collaborative behaviours – Collaborative behaviours are about breaking down silos and building networks, partnerships and eco systems to get work done. Relationships are at the core of these leaders' behaviours and how they spend their time. It is intentional and focused.

Future-fit competencies – You will need to continually add some critical new skills and knowledge to your skills backpack as a leader. You must understand new technology and its impact on society, your industry, and your business; you need to understand how to solve complex, messy problems; you need to understand human-centred design and agile ways of working. These are all critical to the future of work. You also need to understand the more human side of leadership: storytelling and coaching. There is a myriad more, but I start by giving you a few critical ones I continually see as I work with different organisations and leaders.

CHAPTER 5

A New Way Of Thinking About Leadership Development (LD)

Leadership and learning are indispensable to each other.

John F. Kennedy

Leadership development is a lifelong journey, not a quick trip.

John C. Maxwell

I am so tired of debating whether leaders are born or made. Leadership CAN be learned. It is a practice, not a position. And it is a great responsibility. The emergence of mindset research brain theory and habits/practices and adult development approaches bring a better understanding of how we learn and develop over time. People become leaders by practice and by performing deliberate acts of leadership. They learn by making mistakes and trying new things. LD must disrupt the current heroic myths and leadership, the cult of individual achievement and leadership as inherently good and include critical perspectives on how leaders can go astray.

To be a leader, you must like and care about people and want to lead. Therefore, carefully examine your motives and be willing to invest the time and make an effort. Great leaders often spend five hours per week doing deliberate learning. Learning is a habit for them. Did you know our brain gets a dopamine hit from information, learning and new information? Once we get those learning habits going, it becomes addictive.

My research shows that LD needs to focus less on content and methods and more on the context, dynamic process, and learning conditions to become more impactful. Very few leadership development programs address vertical development. As Cook-Greuter (2004) writes, most are geared towards expanding and deepening our current way of making meaning in the world. It is mostly made up of skills, behaviours, and competencies. Vertical development focuses on changing perspectives. People respond to the level they can make meaning of things which might be at a more linear or a more systemic level. If we want to develop leaders that can lead in increased complexity, we need to help them to transform their meaning making systems to include more evolved perspectives that moves beyond the conventional cultural social ceiling or current organisational cultural norms.

Leadership development should focus on helping leaders navigate increasing complexity and stimulate real-time learning that maximises engagement, promotes agility and leads to horizontal and vertical growth. Whether you are developing and starting an organisational leadership development program or developing your own leadership development journey (most of us will do both), you need to heed six factors to be context-informed and impactful. These are shown in Figure 9.

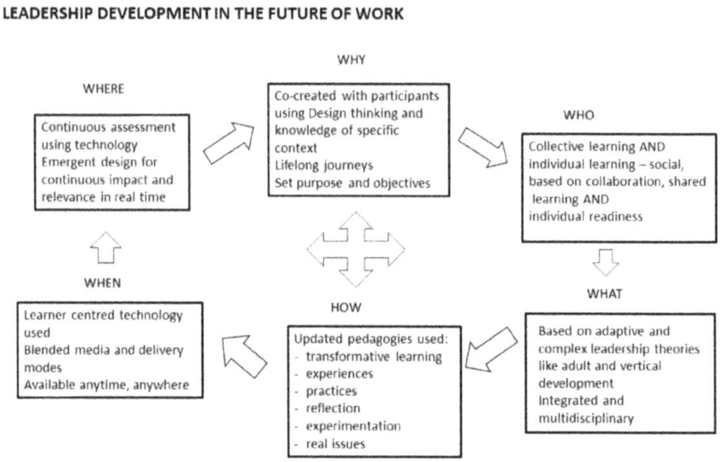
LEADERSHIP DEVELOPMENT IN THE FUTURE OF WORK
WHY
Co-created with participants using Design thinking and knowledge of specific context
Lifelong journeys
Set purpose and objectives
WHERE
Continuous assessment using technology
Emergent design for continuous impact and relevance in real time
WHO
Collective learning AND individual learning – social, based on collaboration, shared learning AND individual readiness
WHEN
Learner centred technology used
Blended media and delivery modes
Available anytime, anywhere
HOW
Updated pedagogies used:
- transformative learning
- experiences
- practices
- reflection
- experimentation
- real issues
WHAT
Based on adaptive and complex leadership theories like adult and vertical development
Integrated and multidisciplinary

Figure 9: LD in the future of work

1) **WHY**. Co-creating the design for the specific **context**, strategy and mindset, practice, and skills gaps of leaders. A systems and design-thinking approach to development can have a transformational effect on individuals and organisations by involving participants in the program's design. What are the specific areas that need focus? What are the priorities collectively and individually?

2) **WHO**. Delivering to all leaders and **participants** at scale and pace ongoing using technology-enabled and curated, just in time content, masterclasses, micro learning, real-life and complex problem immersions, coaching, reflection, and application.

3) **WHAT.** Delivering a **learning experience and content** that is transformative and based on adult development theory. Deliver

challenging and engaging learning using experience, reflection and practice and focused on real messy problems in the role and organisation.

4) **HOW.** Using optimal delivery modes to deliver at scale but also curated to individual needs. These include a blend of learning experience platforms, augmented and virtual reality, in person collectively and individually (coaching), on the mobile and just-in-time. Focus on the dynamic process and conditions of learning. Experience and deliberate practice are key parts of effective learning and embedding.

5) **WHEN.** Blend the learning, enable it through technology and measure adjusting the program to ensure it remains effective and impactful. Have a longer-term design but refine and adjust based on what emerges and what changes in the context. Develop teaching, learning and assessment strategies that transcend space and bring together learners in creative ways. engage learners in actively using multiple resources that encourage self-regulated study, problem-solving and collaboration.

6) **WHERE.** In terms of the timeline of delivery, encourage and deliver lifelong learning opportunities. Encourage leaders to be curious and drive their own learning. Ensure that LD is essentially about reconfiguring mental maps – rethinking the maps and models used to make sense of the world. Learning becomes vital and is ongoing. Growth and learning are interacting with mindsets, beliefs, and practices. The right balance is needed between theory and practice. Theories must be constantly changed and adapted to suit changing contexts. Translating theory into practice is an iterative and cumulative process.

Messy realities of organisations full of contradictions, emotions and ambiguities need to be built into development to reflect real life. LD is about enabling leaders to lead in the real world. Theory needs to be mediated through various strategies and tools that increase understanding and enable application. LD should stimulate real-time learning that maximises engagement, promotes agility and leads to horizontal and vertical growth.

Let's look at some real examples from organisations that have embarked on this journey in Table 2.

Table 2. Future fit LD approaches at Moderna and Cap Gemini

Element	Moderna
Context - WHY	Context powers learning – we only use real life examples, processes and actual challenges when we do development. People are working when they are learning. We use some theory for example when there is a new framework that is important, but we make it practical and real and learning in the flow of work. People want to participate in learning that is real. Our big vision is to be *that* University – we do not just want to be there for our employees – we want to *Transform Human Health*. So, we want to engage the eco system – healthcare providers, patients, regulatory agencies, institutes of health – we want to create a university that pushes out to the world. We have a lot of information that could benefit the world – our science, our manufacturing, supply chain, how we go to market, how we engage customers, how we organise and how we invest.

Element	Moderna
Participants - WHO	We do not have cohorts that migrate through the same program at the same pace and time. We do however segment our population and target certain experiences to certain groups.
Learning experience and content - WHAT	We use our Moderna mindsets and real organisational challenges and processes as the content. 1. We act with urgency 2. We pursue options in parallel 3. We accept risk 4. We obsess over learning 5. We pivot fearlessly 6. We question convention 7. We push past possible 8. We behave like owners 9. We act with dynamic range 10. We remove viscosity 11. We prioritise the platform 12. We digitise everywhere possible We work with Kegan and Lahey's Immunity to Change framework and it underpins everything. We are early in this stage. It is tough for scientists and deep experts. Integrity is top of mind – part of what we call base camp. It is part of our DNA. You can use real Ethical challenges and Moral dilemmas to develop leader ability and understanding. We teach people how to hold paradoxes. We teach people to have dynamic range and make choices all the time.

Element	Moderna
Mode of delivery - HOW	We have speakers, professors, LXP with content libraries, self-directed learning, small groups and nano learning. We look for incremental 1% better improvements all the time, like Olympic Athletes. We cannot master leadership in easy, quick ways or in 3,4 or 5 days. That is not how learning and high performance happens.
Measured and adjusted - WHEN	We try to launch as fast as we can, we do not chase perfection, we chase value. It is experimental and iterative. You learn as you go, and you use data to tell you what is creating an impact and what is not.
Timeline and technology - WHERE	There is no program you start and finish – you belong to different academies where there is ongoing learning – manager, executive, commercial, R&D, CMC academy. What is liberating about how we think about leadership development is that we do not think about it as a linear process. Once you accept that it is iterative and adaptive, it opens up many more possibilities. Your learners can design, iterate and implement with you.

Element	Cap Gemini
Context - WHY	We have incredible potential as a business to really help the entire economy across industries to transition into the digital economy. To make any of this happen, we are a heavily talent dependent business. Without talent, we have no business. So, the disruptions that we've experienced in the talent market made it very obvious that this will require a different type of leadership in terms of navigating the new level of disruption and change. To deal with this context, we co-created a Capgemini leadership vision. We knew that we already had a strong focus on performance, and that we needed to balance that with a focus on the future. We also needed to have the client at the centre of what we do. And to deliver all of this we needed to be aligned and collaborative as well as attract, motivate, and retain the best talent. But we also know we are not one-size-fits-all. Not everyone is going to be excellent at all of these leadership vision elements.
Participants - WHO	Top 2000 leaders.

Element	Cap Gemini
Learning experience and content - WHAT	We use our leadership principles at the core of our learning. These were co-created with our people. 1. Performance Drivers 2. Aligned Entrepreneurs 3. Client Value Creators 4. Talent Magnets 5. Future Shapers These are all paradoxical, so it is critical that we help leaders hold paradoxes.
Mode of delivery - HOW	We kicked off the development work with 360 assessments on the new leadership framework for our EVP's - the top 350 (in parallel with signing off the model). This was supported by coaching afterwards. We then created the VP 360 for the remaining 1600. We made this very, very simple. We showed people the model and then we ask them three questions: 1) What in the context of this leadership vision would you call out as the key three strengths that you see this leader have? 2) How can this person increase their leadership impact in the context of our leadership vision? and 3) What other advice do you have from a career development perspective for this individual? Yesterday, one of our executives, actually said the 360 is so brilliant. It's so quick. "Takes me 10-15 minutes max to respond. But my people love the feedback, the richness that they're getting so purely qualitative, no scoring" In parallel, we have built an on-demand landing page on our Degreed platform where we have curated content in relation to the leadership dimensions - podcasts, little videos, and other bite sized content. Then we have master classes that are more like a deep dive skill booster in different areas. Finally, we are launching in depth training – an executive program with Harvard.

Element	Cap Gemini
Measured and adjusted - WHEN	Still in the process of rolling this out, but we use the 360 results as guide.
Timeline and technology WHERE	You can drive your own learning and /or we have developed some bespoke learning journey design with learning sprints for some priority segments. Leaders can sign up for the sprint that's most relevant for them.

Where to Start

Define The Critical Mindset And Practice Gaps And Set 3-4 Goals For 12 Months

You need to prioritise and pace your learning – what are the critical gaps you need to focus on. What are the 3-4 key areas of focus – the highest change magnitude score for the first 12 months of your learning journey? Here is a tool that might be helpful for you to use. This is an example as shown in Table 3.

Mindsets and practices	Future Importance (1-5)	Current Proficiency A (1-5)	Desired Proficiency B (1-5)	GAP B-A	Change Magnitude*
Contextual intelligence	5	3	5	2	10
Personal agility – growth mindset	5	2	4	2	10
Personal agility – self awareness	5	3	5	2	10
Personal agility - grit	5	2	4	2	10
Personal agility – emotional agility	5	3	5	2	10
Personal agility - focus	4	2	4	2	8
Moral maturity and ethical reasoning	4	2	4	2	8
Identity development – expert to strategist	4	2	4	2	8
Collaborative behaviours	4	2	4	2	8
Future fit competencies– digital literacy	5	3	4	1	5
Future fit competencies– story telling	5	3	4	1	5
Etc.	5	3	4	1	5

*Change magnitude stands for the future importance multiplied by the identified proficiency gap. A high score implies large magnitude of change. This should be a priority development area.

Future Importance: Essential = 5; Low = 1

Proficiency: Full proficient = 5; Not proficient = 1

Table 3: Capability map

Spend 8-12 weeks working on one area at a time – learning, reflecting, practicing, and getting feedback. Then move on to another one. After 12 months – reassess and design the next 12-month journey and sprints.

Immunity To Change

Before you start your journey and sprints, you need to do an immunity to change map for each learning area because we are often immune to change until we have uncovered our behaviours and commitments that compete with the ones we want to change. We need to uncover the underlying unconscious assumptions that drive the competing behaviours and commitments. It is like we have our foot on the gas and brake at the same time all the time when we try and change our mindsets and behaviours.

Here is how you complete an Immunity to Change map (shown in Table 4 below). You write your development goal for the development area (in this case, it is about growth mindset). You identify your current habits, behaviours, and practices that work against that goal. You understand the hidden commitment of why you keep doing the opposite of what you want to do. Finally, you consider why you don't want to give up the old behaviours – what do you assume would happen if you changed – that is the big assumption. Now you are ready to start learning.

Improvement goal	Doing/not doing instead	Hidden competing commitments	Big assumption
I need to make and see mistakes as an opportunity to grow	Do everything perfectly, finding all the information before making any decision, acting	It is more important to do things perfectly, than to allow myself to make a mistake	If I don't do everything perfectly, I will not be seen as a high performer that knows everything

Table 4: Example Immunity to Change map

Source: Kegan and Lahey, 2009

To learn more about the Immunity to Change map, please watch Robert Kegan talk about this in the video below:

https://www.youtube.com/watch?v=FFYnVmGu9ZI An evening with Bob Kegan, 14 min

Now you are ready to learn. You know the priority areas, and you know what would stop you from developing.

Learning Journeys And Sprints

I am a fan of creating learning journeys and sprints. Lang (2018) defines a learning journey: "A Learning Journey is a strategic development approach anchored in business strategy, but with practical application. Ideally intended for groups, cohorts and communities of leaders, a Learning Journey takes place over time. It incorporates multiple formal and informal development components into a unique design, which optimizes training investment and maximizes learning stickiness to change behaviours and transform leaders. A learning journey is perfectly tailored to your organisation's leadership style, culture and the specific needs and preferences of the audiences' level of leadership". (p.1) Becoming an effective leader requires a great effort and time commitment. Viewing leadership as a journey helps to keep the focus on continuous development to activate the organisation's strategy.

For example, the organisation and/or individual can select 6 areas of development focus each year and spend 2 months (8-week sprints) developing and experimenting with these new mindsets, practices, skills, and behaviours. This ensures real focus and embedding of mindsets and practices instead of conceptual overload.

Each 8–12-week sprint starts with the development of an "immunity to change" map (Kegan and Lahey), and then 1 hour a week over 8-12 weeks will learn and practice – a lifelong practice and habit – to become better. At least twice a year, a couple of days of full immersion must complement the ongoing learning journeys. This can be coming together with others to map the context of the organisation and solve real complex issues by applying the learning from the sprints.

You then develop your plan of developing the goal over the 8-12 weeks, for 1 hour a week.

Activities can include:

- Do an assessment
- Attend a masterclass or immersion or event in person or online
- Read or listen to a book/article
- Watch YouTube or TedTalk
- Read a case study
- Try out a tool or behaviour
- Have a conversation with someone
- Visit a place or business you want to learn from
- Work on complex projects in the business
- Co-facilitate leadership and other development programs
- Have or become a coach and mentor.
- Take a secondment.

These activities must be planned for 8-12 weeks and added to your diary to ensure you make time. Plan to use the learning on a real challenge and balance the learning between individual and collective and online and in-person learning. At the end of the 8 weeks, look back at the Immunity to Change map and consider how much you have grown.

To help you assess your gaps and plan your development, I will provide definitions and models for each of the six elements in my Leadership fit for the future of work framework. You might already have mastered areas, and it would be worth spending more time in an area of development.

Once you have completed 6 areas of development for 8 weeks each, start with the next 6 or repeat the ones you need to develop and add new tools, workshops, readings, and development methods. Take breaks between sprints for a week or two to give your brain time to rest.

Here is how one leader develops people in the flow of work.

Practical on the job development - Mteto Nyati, Founder of Wazo Investments, BSG Chairman, Eskom Board Member, former Altron Group CEO and former MTN South Africa CEO

"I am a big believer in learning by doing. If you look at the environments where I worked, I had Executive Assistants or high-potential employees working closely with executives so they can understand the reality of the complexity executives are dealing with (in a safe environment). They have no risk, they can see how decisions are made and the consequences of difficult decisions, but they are not making these decisions.

Also, for the people working for you, your role is to develop them. Give them the complex projects and challenges that will stretch them, they will make mistakes, but you can create an environment where you review what happened. For example, "We lost this deal, what happened?" "We made this acquisition, but it is not performing; let's review it. What were some of our assumptions?"

When you review your failures with a learning mindset, you help people understand the flaws of how the decisions were made. Be intentional about this.

Yes, it is good to take people to business schools, but most of the time, I find they are unable to translate their learnings into their real environments. Are they using what the learnt? You, as a leader, must force people to apply the models they have learnt and if they did not go to business schools, teach them the models and tools yourself and help them use them.

Today I was with someone who used to work for me in Altron, and he is so happy that he is flying on his own. I am so happy he is not dependent on me or anyone else. He knows how to apply these models and tools.

Finally, I am always intentional in my leadership role to give complex and problematic projects to young talent and work through it with them. Ask the teams to come and present to the leaders of the business – there is so much learning on both sides."

CHAPTER 6

The Starting Point: Contextual Intelligence

I make sense of and act on the changes around me – CONTEXTUAL INTELLIGENCE

In high uncertainty conditions, you need to plan to learn, not plan to prove you were right. Stop pretending you know all the answers. In a highly uncertain and fluid environment, neither you nor anybody else has answers. Arguing about being 'right' or having a detailed plan going eighteen months out is just wasting your breath. Instead, articulate and pinpoint the major uncertainties and how you might gain some insight about them."

Rita McGrath

Do not simply overlay your existing framework on a new situation. The new situation may be very different. Instead, let the appropriate map or framework emerge from your understanding of the situation.

Deborah Ancona

Today's leaders, managers, and employees must be able to foresee and diagnose any number of changing contexts quickly, then seamlessly adapt to that brand new context or risk becoming obsolete and irrelevant. Diagnosing context successfully requires intentional leadership and a paradoxical devotion to having a global perspective in the midst of local circumstances.

Matthew Kutz

We cannot deal with something if we cannot make sense of it. Evidence shows that threat and fear lead to rigidity and people trying to protect the status quo or even inaction. It can also result in a need for control and direction, treating employees as helpless. It can also lead to erratic behaviour where leaders frantically try one quick fix after another.

So, it is essential to ensure leaders have the right contextual map to navigate the organisation through strategic alignment and renewal. Without a deeper and richer understanding of this disruptive context, leaders will struggle to develop a more robust capacity to reinvent their organisations' business models and processes. Diagnosing context is a leadership skill that transcends specific roles or environments. So, what is the context?

"Context consists of all the external, internal, and interpersonal factors that contribute to the uniqueness of each situation and circumstance. Intelligence is the ability to transform data into useful information, information into knowledge, and then most importantly, assimilate that knowledge into practice... The contextually intelligent person then uses that new knowledge to exert influence in crafting a desirable future." (Kutz,2013, p.5)

There are some models and approaches that are helpful in developing your contextual intelligence. One model comes from Matthew Kutz (2008). He reports that **contextual intelligence** requires "an intuitive grasp of relevant past events, acute awareness of present contextual variables, and awareness of the preferred future" (p. 18). The contextually intelligent person is one who "appropriately interprets and reacts to changing and volatile surroundings"(Kutz, 2010, p. 271). Critical to Kutz's description of contextual intelligence is the understanding that it also includes the ease of movement between different contexts.

The other approach is spotting inflection points. As Rita McGrath puts it - leaders can and must **see around corners**. They should be good at spotting and acting on Inflection points. (McGrath, 2019). A strategic inflection point is a change, typically in the environment, technology, social norms, or many other different things that could cause that. The key insight is that an inflection point causes the taken-for-granted assumptions your business is based on to be no longer true.

A big dramatic **inflection point** has almost always been gestating for a while. The earlier you can spot an inflection point, the easier it is to design a strategy to deal with it. We often only use lagging indicators like operating margins, EBITDA, revenue etc. and over-analyze them instead of current (i.e., operating cash flow, production costs etc. and leading indicators, i.e., employee engagement, management effectiveness, customer love.

According to Professor McGrath (2019), "The real heroes of galvanizing the organization" are typically not the top management. Those with real insights into strategic agility are often the people close to the coal face of the organization … who often have flashes of real insight into what is happening. The senior leadership role is often more about providing a space for those insights to be heard, recognizing the ones that are significant, and empowering those with the most knowledge to do something about them."

Before an organisation can do something about an emerging inflection point, a critical mass of people need to believe that they are at a turning point. If no action is taken now, the future will be dim. Although senior leadership has a role to play in the process of capturing all employees' hearts and minds toward this purpose, the actions of many people, up and down the hierarchy, are what lead to a desirable outcome.

Professor McGrath has various steps that firms can take to spot coming inflection points. They include opening themselves to "critical communication with people who may disagree or who may have different vantage points," and "get out of the building," not closeting themselves with like-minded people. They need to court diversity in terms of viewpoint. They should use small, agile, empowered teams for reversible experimental decisions and encourage "little bets that are rich in learning, ideally distributed across the organization."

When Satya Nadella became the CEO, Microsoft had missed the mobile revolution and was in danger to miss the AI and Cloud inflections. To make Microsoft competitive again, Nadella created a culture of constant learning, bottom-up innovation, and a relentless focus on "customer love". He began executive meetings with presentations on the research team's latest developments and leading indicators (such as product usage).

Elizabeth Lagerstedt writes that inflection points (as shown in Figure 10) may mean you need to change the very assumptions on which your company was founded. In this light, strategic renewal is vital for any business to survive inflection points long-term. Without strategic renewal, a company is destined for decline as it fails to remain relevant and value-adding.

The most important question to answer right now is whether or not you are at an inflection point. And if so, what are you going to do about it?

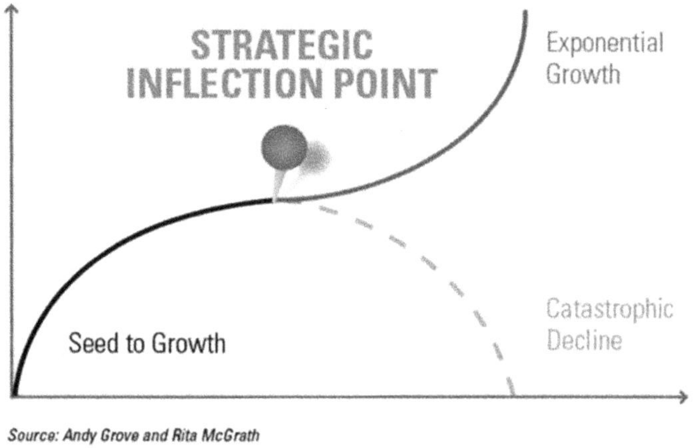
STRATEGIC
INFLECTION POINT
Exponential
Growth
Catastrophic
Decline
Seed to Growth
Source: Andy Grove and Rita McGrath

Figure 10: A strategic inflection point

A final useful frame is that of deliberate **sense-making**. In a business sense, it means learning about shifting markets, customer migration, new technologies, new ways of working and other changes. Sense making enables leaders to better grasp what is going on in their environments, thus helping with other leadership activities such as visioning, relating, and inventing. Sense making involves coming up with plausible understandings and meanings; testing them with others and via action; and then refining our understandings or abandoning them in favour of new ones that better explain a shifting reality. It is critical when the environment changes rapidly and confronts us with unexpected complexity.

By mapping an unfamiliar situation, some fear of the unknown can be abated. It is about developing plausible understandings and meanings, testing them with others, and refining your understanding via small pilots. It means you are looking for a unifying order or a map. By having all members of a team working from a common map of "what's going on out there," coordinated action is facilitated. As we try to map confusion and bring coherence to what seems mysterious, we can talk about what is happening, bring multiple interpretations to our situations, and then act. Sensemaking involves not only trying out new things but also trying to understand your impact on a system as you try to change it. (Ancona, 2012).

What Leaders Say

Gerald Marion Chief Customer and Strategy Officer: Bupa AsiaPac

"Our internal context of Bupa was an ambition to transform to the most customer centric organisation in the world – that is the Group CEO's ambition – but by default we are set up as a P&L business. So, there is the ambition and then there is the reality. As we set ourselves up for the ambition, we needed to understand what customer centricity meant and therefore not just a statement, but a management and leadership system that would enable us to achieve this. The Group CEO had a very clear ambition of several things that needed to come together. It was a systemic transformation – not a linear transformation – and a lot of our leaders were very linear in their approach and driving individual, disconnected objectives. That was one of the first challenges to recognise. The parts needed to work together to achieve what we called "The Elephant" strategy, 3 x 6. Our Group CEO talked about Bupa being a sleeping elephant, but when an elephant is active and charging nothing can stop. It goes at 18km an hour – 3 x 6 – so we had 3 ambitions and 6 pillars which was a system.

Our external context had 3 things we needed to respond to. 1) customers wanted to be much more empowered in their decision making – people don't think about "how is my health insurance, or dentist going", they think about "how am I going to live my best life today". There was a disconnect between what they wanted and what we were providing, which were products. 2) we could see how digital innovation was reshaping health care – new technology, virtual care,

AI etc. but unless we were more connected into this eco system and aligned in delivery, we would lose a great opportunity. This was already showing up in slower growth. 3) the "uberisation" of healthcare – in the current environment you must come to me as a provider, whereas "uberisation" was about the democratisation of health care. We needed to align ourselves and our skills sets to this new context. For example, we needed more systems thinkers rather than linear thinkers. We also got a lot more data and we needed to get the data together to create a participatory health care model. We needed to become an integrated health care provider that has trust at the heart of the experience that empowers the customer around human outcomes. We asked 1) How do we empower the customer to be more connected and make the right choices? 2) How do we ensure customers and employees feel loved and valued? This had to come before we looked at technology and data.

ESG is also super important for us because there is only One Planet and therefore One Health. So, during the bushfires in Australia in 2019 and 2020, we saw that a lot of people's health being affected. And as floods and fires continued, we saw an increasing correlation between the environment and the health of people. We needed to become a far more active player in protecting the health of the planet if we wanted to care of the health of the people. Our strategic intent and priorities reflect this."

Mteto Nyati, Founder of Wazo Investments, BSG Chairman, Eskom Board Member, former Altron Group CEO and former MTN South Africa CEO

"Context matters and we are living in an environment today where there is so much rapid change. There is change in almost all dimensions of human life. For example, because of COVID we have introduced remote work. That in its own is a leader challenge because you are used to having people around you. How do you continue to look after people that are not with you, how do you connect with them? There is a challenge around ESG – we need to move away from emissions as fast as possible, but some companies are right in those industries and how do they move forward without shedding jobs?

In South Africa, people feel like we have so much coal. Why are we thinking about renewables? But it is harming the environment – so we need to help people to understand the need for change. The issues in South Africa of gender based violence and crime in the workplace you must deal with. I used to be on the Board of Walmart (Massmart), and it is horrifying to hear about rape in the workplace, but it reflects the society we live in. You must deal with this as a leader.

There is also a dimension of race – we are still so much where people look at differences and see it as a threat rather than an opportunity to innovate.

I call this dynamic complexity rather than detailed complexity. Detailed complexity is the volume of stuff, dynamic is that things are changing so fast. To deal with dynamic complexity, one must understand deeply the connection and interrelatedness between things. Systems thinking is critical for good leadership."

Catherine Clark – CEO Paralympics Australia

"I work at the complex intersection as a female leader with Sport and Disability overlayed with First Nation reparation. It is extremely complex to make sense of it all.

More generally, we are facing more wicked problems than ever before as leaders. The way people show up for work and how they feel about work has changed forever and we cannot lead the way we led before. Learning and unlearning is the new currency."

Brid Horan – Chancellor Dublin City University, Independent Chair and Non-Executive Director, Founding member 30% Club Ireland

"The way I make sense of the complex and ever-changing environment is to read, talk to different people, listen to podcasts and create small experiments. I also try and work in and expose myself to different sectors and issues and learn from all the different issues I work with in my different roles."

Dee McGrath – CEO Link Group, Board member – Chief Executive Women, Revolut Australia

Dee is another leader who is a prolific learner. When I asked her how she makes time to and how she makes sense of the changing and complex environment, she told me:

"I read and listen to podcasts – on the plane, in the car, before I go to sleep. I read and listen broadly – about industry shifts, business model changes, growth mindset, high performance, and wellness. I talk to people with different views and try and stay open to their perspectives."

Is This A Gap For You?

1. Do you embrace complexity?
2. Are you future focused?
3. Do you read, talk to others, listen to thought and industry leaders and conduct research to make sense of the contextual changes?
4. Do you look for an act on inflection points?
5. Do you proactively deal with and respond to trends and changes in the context?

Insight

Set Your Goal And Develop Your Immunity To Change Map

Improvement goal	Doing/not doing instead	Hidden competing commitments	Big assumption

RESOURCES

Books

SEEING
AROUND
CORNERS
Rita McGrath

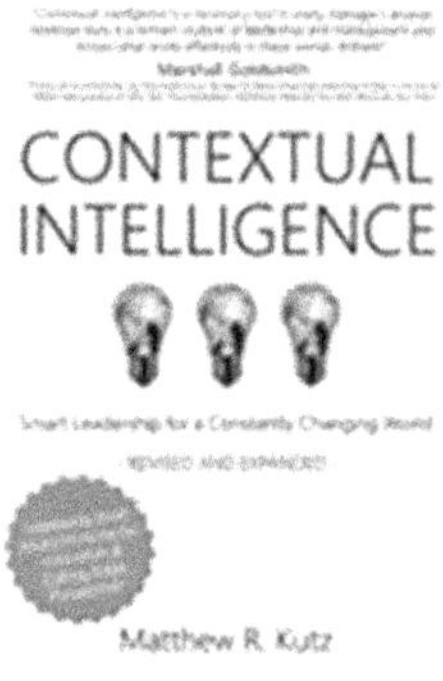
CONTEXTUAL
INTELLIGENCE
Matthew R. Kutz

Articles

https://hbr.org/2007/02/in-praise-of-the-incomplete-leader

https://www.obforum.com/article/

creating-early-warnings-scenarios-rita-mcgrath

https://www.regent.edu/acad/global/publications/rgbr/vol2iss2/RGBR_Vol_2_Issue_2_PDF.pdf

Video Clips And Podcasts

https://www.youtube.com/watch?v=MxHMDhSdTIU 30 min Rita McGrath

https://www.ritamcgrath.com/podcast/

CHAPTER 7

The Enabler: Personal Agility

I thrive in complexity
and uncertainty
PERSONAL AGILITY
AND CURIOSITY

When faced with continual complexity at unprecedented pace, our survival instincts kick in. In a mental panic to regain control, we fight, flee, or freeze: we act before thinking ("we've got to make some kind of decision, now!"), we analyze an issue to the point of paralysis, or we abdicate responsibility by ignoring the problem or shunting it off to a committee or task force. We need inner agility, but our brain instinctively seeks stasis. At the very time that visionary, empathetic, and creative leadership is needed, we fall into conservative, rigid old habits.

McKinsey Quarterly

We are not thriving at the moment. Amy Cohen (2023) shares research that recently found 54% of C-suite leaders falling into the "always-on" trap with subsequent burnout on the rise. Pressure to perform and adapt will not disappear but we need to make some different choices.

Almost half of the time, we operate on "automatic pilot" or unconscious of what we are doing or how we feel, as our mind wanders to somewhere else other than here and now. In addition to the constant mind-wandering, the various cognitive biases and beliefs also affect our ability to have a correct understanding of ourselves.

But we cannot be impeded by our old beliefs, as these old mentalities do not inspire growth and adaptability. We cannot expect the same rules or actions to apply across the multitude of experiences and circumstances we go through in our lives. A seed cannot grow from concrete, only from a mixture of fertile soil, water, and sunlight.

Lucky for us, behaviour is learnt, and our brains can change. We can unlearn and relearn better ways of being and doing. It is possible for a person to move from making unconscious choices to making more courageous, bold, and deliberate conscious choices that transform the result they are seeking. You can learn to make these conscious choices that will not only create an enormous positive and abundant ripple effect, but also more important, sustain the success achieved.

Most of what you need is already inside you. You can build the key mindsets and practices of Personal Agility. You do this by re-aligning your mindsets, actions, emotions, and thoughts to your values and become more conscious of your behaviour. In my work over the last 28 years, I understand what drives "thriving" – it comes down to consistently applying six mindsets and practices. These are:

Growth Mindset – showing up with curiosity and the belief that you and others can grow and develop continually.

Self-Awareness - internal self-awareness - how clearly, we see our own values, passions, aspirations, fit with our environment, reactions, and impact on others and the second - external self-awareness - understanding how other people view us, in terms of those same factors listed above. (Eurich, 2018).

Emotional agility - understanding all your emotions—negative and positive—and aligning your decisions and actions intentionally.

Focus and Deep Work - Your focus is your reality. Attention works like a muscle. We learn, interact and work best with focused attention and presence, but the wealth of information and distractions creates a poverty of attention. We need to learn to carve out time for focused deep work and starve our distractions.

Grit - the right blend of passion and perseverance has been shown repeatedly to be the key differentiator of long-term success across several studies.

Let's help you understand and develop these mindsets and practices. The cornerstone mindset must be a growth mindset and curiosity – it is the door to learning and growing.

PERSONAL AGILITY PRACTICE 1:

GROWTH MINDSET

Great leaders are curious. They want to try new things, experience the world and learn from others. Their curiosity fuels their intellect.

Simon Sinek

At its core, a growth mindset is about human motivation and curiosity. Curious people ask a lot of questions, seek new experiences and they are willing to make mistakes. If you have a growth mindset, you believe that even if you struggle with certain skills, your abilities aren't set in stone. You think that with work, your skills can improve over time. If we believe our own others' abilities are static, we have a fixed mindset. We believe no matter how hard we try; we will not learn or improve and avoid challenges and stick to things we have mastered. We believe we are born with fixed intelligence and talent.

When we have a growth mindset, we believe intelligence and talent can develop over time through effort and action.

According to Carol Dweck's Mindset Theory, we all fall along a spectrum regarding our implicit beliefs. We usually have a mix of mindsets and beliefs – in some things, we have a growth mindset, and some a fixed mindset. Fixed mindset has two sides – either fear – being wrong, looking stupid OR arrogance – I am the expert, I know the answers. Growth mindset takes a fresh and optimistic look at things and says: I can learn this, I can see new aspects I have not thought about before, this is a great challenge, even though it did not work out this time, I have learnt a lot. (Dweck, 2008).

To develop a growth mindset, you should not let setbacks keep you from wanting or working to learn and improve. Identify your fixed mindset triggers that inhibit our growth – this might include your response to criticism or comparing yourself to others. We need to work on the basic beliefs and views of ourselves and others. Failure does not define you – it presents a learning opportunity. It is temporary and changeable.

Language is critical. Challenging yourself and the team to use "not yet" rather than "we cannot do this", asking "what are we going to try next?", "what can we do differently?" all drive growth mindset outcomes. Set up a failure board and track your learning from each one. Set up experiments. Encourage the team to take on tough challenges. Reward effort and learning.

Curiosity is a journey to a growth mindset. Did you know your brain rewards you for being curious? It increases your dopamine levels! So be willing to ask questions and drive your learning intentionally. Our desire to learn should be a constant. It should be an ongoing practice, especially amid uncertainty. Slow down, ask questions, and listen.

When entire companies embrace a growth mindset, employees report feeling more empowered and committed and they collaborate and innovate more. How much do you, as a leader, enable your teams to embrace a growth mindset in their daily business? Do you live and breathe curiosity and a growth mindset? Here are examples of leaders and organisations who make growth mindset and curiosity part of their DNA and culture.

Microsoft decided growth mindset should be at the core of its culture. Inspired by Professor Carol Dweck, Nadella and Kathleen Hogan, Microsoft CHRO and the senior leadership team determined that a growth mindset would become the foundation of Microsoft's desired-toward culture. A range of approaches have since been taken to start and drive efforts for long-term change, starting with engaging senior leaders to talk about and role model growth mindset, employee-awareness campaigns to drive growth mindset adoption, and ongoing measurement of how the employees experience growth mindset in the company.

For example, interactive online modules with rich storytelling and multimedia were created for employees to learn about growth mindset. Conversation guides were built for managers to enable meaningful exchanges about growth mindset behaviors in team settings. Leaders also engage in storytelling to give examples of growth mindset behaviours.

Successes with demonstrated growth mindset behaviours are celebrated as reinforcements of growth mindset habits in the workplace. Various employee engagement and training solutions like games, quizzes, lending libraries with curated books, mobile empathy museum, and creative environmental assets were developed to engage employees around growth mindset behaviours.

One of the essential efforts was developing Microsoft leadership principles, in partnership with NLI, with the intent of engaging everyone in the company – from senior executives to new hires – in building growth mindset habits, processes, and environment into everyday culture experience at Microsoft.

Daily pulse surveys constantly collect metrics of employee experiences of growth mindset, more detailed items such as levels of risk aversion, visibly recognizing and learning from failure, or support in unlocking one's ability. Let's see how one leader at Microsoft brings this to life in his mindsets and practices.

Brian Murphy – Senior Director, Employee Skilling, Microsoft
Brian, like the rest of Microsoft, is a strong believer in curiosity and having a growth mindset. He also believes in continuous and collaborative learning. To improve his leadership, he seeks feedback on his leadership practice and asks for coaching and mentoring to help him grow – this includes him being a mentor to younger leaders. He uses after-action reviews, journaling and peer coaching as tools. He also works hard to maintain his professional networks.

Novartis believes that curiosity drives discovery and innovation and solves problems. They strive to provide the best learning opportunities to spark curiosity. They set learning as an intention and encourage each associate to devote 5% (100 hours a year) of their time learning and developing skills. They also bring together communities throughout the year to debate and discuss issues. Simon Brown, the Chief Learning Officer of Novartis, wrote a book called *The Curious Advantage*. He explains how important curiosity is, how they fuel it in the organisation, and how they embed it in the culture through learning and experimentation. In 2020, for example, Novartis ran a Curiosity Month, an integrated learning experience of 180 events and over 45,000 learning hours.

https://www.novartis.com/about/strategy/people-and-culture/ we-are-instilling-curiosity

I have been further struck by how leaders who thrive in the future of work context are curious and comfortable with mistakes and learning as a normal part of being a leader. Giam Swiegers and Gerald Marion are great examples of this.

Giam Swiegers – Chairman, Aurecon, former Group CEO, Aurecon, Former CEO Deloitte Australia

"One of my strongest leader attributes is my intellectual curiosity. I am forever looking out in the market for new thinking and ideas and introducing them to the organisation. I find if you have hired smart people, there is always someone that has also heard of it and is interested to take it further.

My biggest mistake is that I hung onto bad or poor performing people for too long. My natural inclination is to want to change them, and this took me a long time to realise it never works. Now that I am in an advisory and Chairman roles, it is the thing I say most to the leadership teams. "You know so and so is not working out. Stop wasting time. Offer them something attractive to leave the organisation but get them out as soon as possible". I don't think I ever got rid of people on time, and it harms your reputation because people ask why you are not dealing with the underperformer or cultural misfit. Luckily, I had an individual on my team that was very good at it. It is important to balance your strengths with those of others."

Gerald Marion – Chief Customer and Strategy Officer, BUPA Australia

"I work on the principle that every 3 years I need to reset and relearn. So, I invest in myself and my studies every 3 years. Covid was hard because there was no time. But when I was transitioning from consulting into a senior corporate role, I did a 2-year course at MIT on Regional Entrepreneurship and Innovation Acceleration. I then apply the techniques and lessons in my work.

Now I am mindful that after our first phase of the transformation, I believe we need a new playbook. That is why I went onto mentoring with former CEOs. It is all conversation based and knowledge being passed on. It is like being an apprentice. I am also attending the Corporate Director Course to consolidate the previous experience and learnings I had. It was the same with the MIT course. I was doing a lot of the work, but I wanted to test and solidify my knowledge and experience.

I noticed that colleagues who did not develop themselves came into the transformation with their old tools and thinking. We were therefore not aligned on language and ways forward. They struggled most with having a dual mindset – how to run and optimise the business whilst building the future and the foundations of the future to remain competitive."

Is This A Gap For You?

Take the Mindset quiz below in the link.

https://blog.mindsetworks.com/what-s-my-mindset

Insight

Set Your Goal And Develop Your Immunity To Change Map

Improvement goal	Doing/not doing instead	Hidden competing commitments	Big assumption

RESOURCES

Books

MILLION-COPY BESTSELLER
mindset
Changing the way you think to fulfil your potential

THE GREATEST DRIVER OF VALUE IN THE DIGITAL AGE
THE CURIOUS ADVANTAGE

Articles

https://hbr.org/2016/01/what-having-a-growth-mindset-actually-means

https://hbr.org/2018/09/the-business-case-for-curiosity

https://hbr.org/2018/09/curiosity)

Video Clips And Podcasts

The power of believing that you can improve by Carol Dweck 11:00

https://www.youtube.com/watch?v=jrZev2Y37ZQ podcast 19 min Carol Dweck

https://www.youtube.com/watch?v=cFLf2pX0mSA How does Novartis nurture learning curiosity? 3:42

PERSONAL AGILITY PRACTICE 2:

SELF-AWARENESS

Leadership is courageous, authentic influence that creates enduring value.

Leaders either shed light or cast shadow on everything they do. It comes from our values, traits, principles, life experiences, beliefs, motives, and essence. Leadership is an intimate expression of who we are; it is our whole person in action.

Kevin Cashman

A lack of self-awareness can alienate others through misunderstanding the impact of your actions on them. The Arbinger Institute found that human beings have little comprehension of what we are. The difficulty is not that we are ignorant. It's that we are self-deceiving. We systematically avoid understanding ourselves. (Warner, 2019).

A study by the Cornell School of Industrial and Labour Relations found self-awareness the strongest predictor of overall success. (Flaum, 2018), Awareness of one's own weaknesses enables executives to work with others differing strengths to them; they can more easily accept the idea someone else may have better ideas or abilities than their own.

Kevin Cashman believed we lead by virtue of who we are. He encourages leaders to break free from self-limiting patters, to extract learning from every experience and every feedback opportunity and continue evolving ourselves. It is a lifelong commitment to self-discovery and self-observation. Understand the software that runs your leadership. Does it need an upgrade? He says:

- To grow we have to explore our belief systems and the software that is running our leadership.
- We have Conscious Beliefs (explicit, known) and Shadow Beliefs (subtler, more challenging to uncover i.e., exceptionally high standards).
- Transforming Shadow Beliefs to Conscious Beliefs is critical to personal mastery.
- Leaders either shed light or cast shadow on everything they do. The more conscious their self-awareness, the more light leaders bring. The more limited their self-understanding, the bigger the shadow a leader casts.

Fortunately, self-awareness can evolve and develop over time. We can become aware of our values, feelings, thoughts, strengths, our blind spots, our triggers, our reactions and our habits and mindsets and we can work to change them. Self-awareness is a prerequisite for identity development we will discuss later in more detail. We develop self-awareness through introspection, ongoing development, and focused attention. (Carden et al, 2022). Building self-awareness is about self-improvement and self-management.

Tasha Eurich (2018) has done significant research into what self-awareness is and how to cultivate it. She found that even though most people believe they are self-aware, it is rare. Only 10-15% of people fit the self-awareness criteria they designed. They define two types of self-awareness. The first is internal self-awareness – how we see our own values, passions, aspirations, fit with our environment, reactions, strengths, and impact on others. The second is external self-awareness

– our understanding of how other people view us regarding the same factors. People skilled at seeing themselves like others do are better at empathy and relationships. Leaders need to work on both types. Senior leaders need to do more work than others as they get less honest feedback.

https://hbr.org/2018/01/what-self-awareness-really-is-and-how-to-cultivate-it

True North: Discover Your Authentic Leadership (2007) by Bill George with Peter Sims drew on interviews with 125 leaders, aged 23 to 93, selected mainly due to their reputations for authenticity and effectiveness as leaders. At the time it constituted the largest in-depth study of leadership development. The idea was to learn how these people developed their leadership abilities. Early on, however, the authors note: 'Analysing 3,000 pages of transcripts, our team was startled to see that these people did not identify any universal characteristics, traits, skills, or styles that led to their success'.

Instead, asserts George, their leadership abilities emerged from their life stories. 'Consciously and subconsciously, they were constantly testing themselves through real-world experiences and reframing their life stories to understand who they were at their core. In doing so, they discovered the purpose of their leadership and learned that being authentic made them more effective,' he says.

Let's look at a leader that works from a level of continuous reflection and self-insight.

Vas Narasimhan, the CEO of Novartis, is a great example of a leader with high levels of self-awareness. He is conscious of his impact and energy and works on self-discipline and a series of habits. He says he does not always get it right, but he tries to be consistent. Some habits he calls out to have a positive, purposeful, present mindset include:

- "I meditate most days using an app, and I try to reflect on my personal vision: "Improve myself, inspire a healthier world."
- "I monitor my self-talk for going "below the line." It can mean the difference between living in a world of fight or flight versus a world of possibilities."
- "I always try to remind myself of these three things that make people (including me) unhappy: worrying about things we cannot control, creating drama out of the little things (and most things in life are little), and not being fully present."

https://www.linkedin.com/pulse/managing-my-energy-time-vas-narasimhan/

At an organisational level, **Novartis** creates an unbossed environment. They focus on developing leaders who are self-aware and self-curious. Vas, the CEO, works with Jennifer Garvey Berger as a coach to help him develop self-awareness and empathy. He calls himself "a work in progress" and a "student of leadership"

Another leader I have always admired for her self-awareness, curiosity, grit, and courage is Catherine Clark.

Catherine Clark – CEO Paralympics Australia

"I am not defined by my title or status. I have always been curious, wanting to learn, wanting to make the people around me successful. This awareness of my leadership came about when I played sport (hockey) at a competitive level – I had to choose between hockey and tennis – and I chose hockey because it was about the team not the individual. I played in the centre where I could calm people and direct the traffic."

Is This A Gap For You?

Take the self-awareness test in the link below.

https://www.insight-book.com/quiz

Insight

Set Your Goal And Develop Your Immunity To Change Map

Improvement goal	Doing/not doing instead	Hidden competing commitments	Big assumption

RESOURCES

Books

HOW TO SUCCEED BY
SEEING YOURSELF CLEARLY
INSIGHT
DR TASHA EURICH

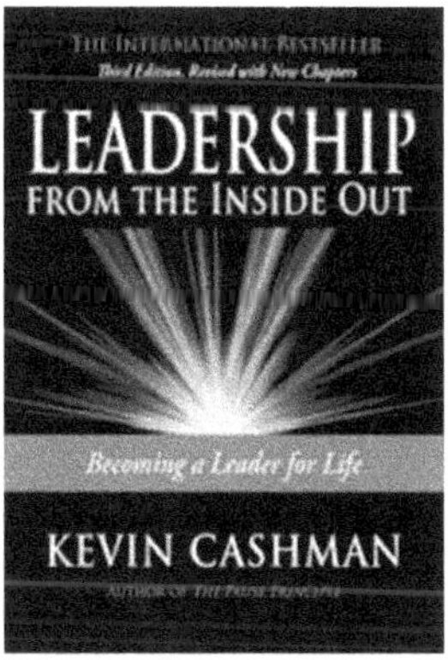
LEADERSHIP
FROM THE INSIDE OUT
Becoming a Leader for Life
KEVIN CASHMAN

Articles

https://hbr.org/2018/01/

what-self-awareness-really-is-and-how-to-cultivate-it

https://hbr.org/2018/10/working-with-people-who-arent-self-aware
https://hbr.org/2019/06/

how-to-move-from-self-awareness-to-self-improvement

https://hbr.org/2015/02/5-ways-to-become-more-self-aware

Video Clips And Podcasts

https://www.youtube.com/watch?v=dU7Wm-FcXvc&t=21s 44 min Tasha Eurich

https://www.youtube.com/channel/UCsJ8bEQ-O4dFCjePSeOr68Q Kevin Cashman - various

PERSONAL AGILITY PRACTICE 3:

GRIT

A gritty individual sets long-term goals for themselves and doesn't waver on them even in the absence of positive feedback.

Angela Duckworth

Grit isn't about luck, talent, or positive thinking, but having deeper goals and values that gives meaning to your work and fighting to attain those goals.

Ari Zoldan

The happiest people wake up every day to hard goals.

Caroline Adam Miller

Achieving anything worthwhile requires effort, and you will face obstacles. Grit is about perseverance and passion for long-term goals. Grit is sticking with your future, day in and day out, and not just for the week, the month, or the years. High achievers have extraordinary stamina. Even at the top of their game, they strive to improve. Even when their work requires sacrifice, they remain in love with what they do. Even when easier paths beckon, their commitment is steadfast. This is what we call "grit". That means grit is living life like a marathon, not a sprint. Develop grit without burning out. The opposite of grit is the inability to sustain focus or energy in pursuing purposeful goals that improve yourself and the world.

Angela Duckworth (2017) came up with the idea of Grit. Duckworth's research on grit has shown that…

- West Point cadets who scored highest on the Grit Test were 60% more likely to succeed than their peers.
- Ivy League undergraduate students with more grit also had higher GPAs than their peers even though they had lower SAT scores and weren't as "smart."
- When comparing two people of the same age but with different levels of education, grit (and not intelligence) more accurately predicts which one will be better educated.
- Competitors in the National Spelling Bee outperform their peers not because of IQ but because of their grit and commitment to more consistent practice.

There are 5 mindsets and practices that make up grit:

1. **Perseverance** – a continued effort to do or achieve something despite the difficulty. It is about not giving up.
2. **Resilience** – the ability to bounce back when we fail or face tough challenges. It is about quick recovery and self-care.
3. **Courage** is about the courage to do new and hard things and be willing to fail twice on the way. The desire to learn and achieve is greater than the fear.
4. **Passion** is about understanding what is important to you and creating short- and long-term goals to achieve this. It must be rooted in your values. Passion is the foundation of grit.
5. **Conscientiousness** comes from planning and discipline to stay motivated and follow through.

https://www.betterup.com/blog/to-be-great-grit-isnt-all-that-matters

Gritty people work in a way that evokes the Zeigarnik effect, so they always have unfinished goals pulling them forward. This theory comes from Bluma Zeigarnik, a researcher who noticed that waiters in a restaurant still trying to complete a diner's order could recall the details of that order, while waiters who had successfully finished their work with a table couldn't recall the details of the order they had just delivered. Zeigarnik refined these initial observations through various tests until she finally concluded those working toward a goal who code it as completed in their minds don't then have a restlessness that drives them to continue working on the goal. However, people who don't quit at goals always have something whirring in the background of their minds, whether they're trying to figure out how to solve a problem, find the right resources, or search for new ways to succeed.

It's not enough to be gritty about everything. People with authentic grit have a passion for something. When you have a powerful "why" behind what you are doing and are intrinsically motivated to do this difficult thing because it is important to you, not necessarily to anyone else, you will instinctively be pulled back to what is unfinished. The other reason it works so well is that when people expect to do well with their goals—when they have high hope and robust self-efficacy—they return to create completion. So, a sure test of whether you are truly motivated to achieve a goal is if you respond to unfinished business with passion, curiosity, and zest. If not, you might not be pursuing a gritty goal right for you.

https://waiyancan.com/summary-getting-grit-by-caroline-adams-miller/?utm_content=cmp-true

According to Angela Duckworth, grit is about holding the same top-level goal for a long time. Visualize your goal setting as a hierarchy with multiple levels as shown in Figure 9.

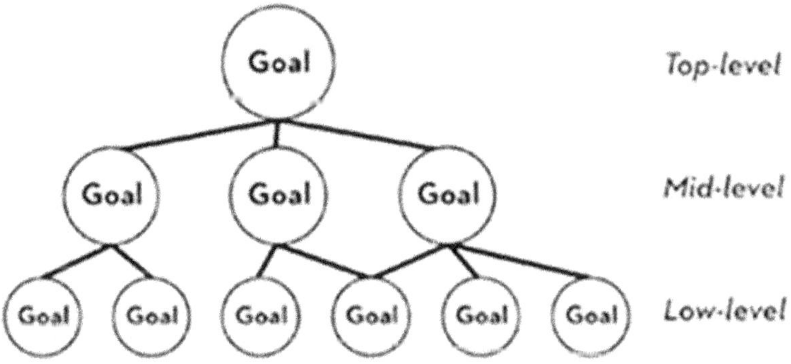
Goal
Top-level
Goal
Goal
Goal
Mid-level
Goal
Goal
Goal
Goal
Goal
Goal
Low-level

Figure 9: A hierarchy of goals

The low-level goals are your day-to-day actions like writing emails, attending meetings, jogging for an hour, reading, etc. We do these goals as a means to an end of a higher-level goal - such as executing a project. The higher the goal in this hierarchy, the more abstract, general, and important it is. Waking up at 6 am is a low-level goal. It only matters because of a mid-level goal, arriving to work on time. Let's look at a real-life example of grit.

Toby Cosgrove the CEO of Cleveland Clinic had dyslexia, undiagnosed until his mid-thirties, with a poor academic record. He applied to 13 medical schools, being accepted by only one. He joined a clinic in 1975, achieving major results for the rest of this career:

- Performed more cardiac surgeries (about 22,000) than any others.
- Pioneered several technologies and innovations earning over 30 patents.

  Named CEO in 2004. In addition to the improvements in patient experience, revenue grew from $3.7 billion in 2004 to $8.5 billion in 2016, and total annual visits increased from 2.8 million to 7.1 million.

- On virtually every available metric, quality rose to the top tier of U.S. health care.
- A placard on his desk reminds him, "What can be conceived can be created."

Is This A Gap For You?

Complete the Grit Scale

https://angeladuckworth.com/grit-scale/

Insight

Set Your Goal And Develop Your Immunity To Change Map

Improvement goal	Doing/not doing instead	Hidden competing commitments	Big assumption

RESOURCES

Books

#1 NEW YORK TIMES BESTSELLER
GRIT
Why passion and resilience are the secrets to success
Angela Duckworth

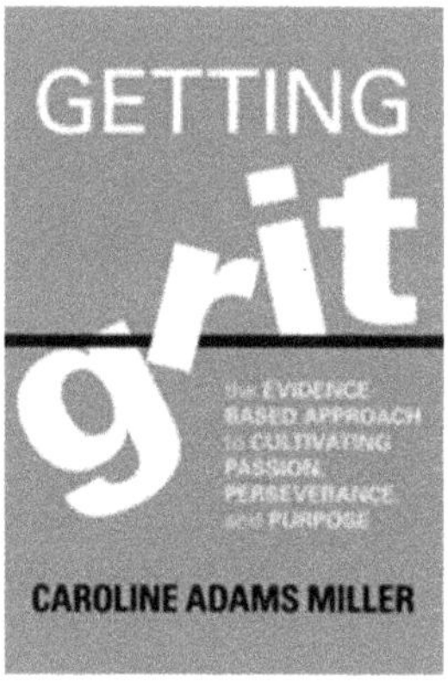
GETTING
grit
CAROLINE ADAMS MILLER

Articles

https://jamesclear.com/grit

https://blogs.cfainstitute.org/investor/2022/07/15/ angela-duckworth-the-power-of-grit/

Video Clips And Podcasts

The power of passion and perseverance by Angela Duckworth (6:00)

https://americanradioworks.publicradio.org/features/tomorrows-college/grit/angela-duckworth-grit.html 53 mins

https://www.youtube.com/watch?v=mRqBI5gy3Gs Caroline Adams Miller: Grit and Goals 9 min

https://vimeo.com/250654148 Angela Duckworth: Hierarchy of Goals 2 min

PERSONAL AGILITY PRACTICE 4: EMOTIONAL AGILITY

Leaders are always expected to be "in control"—so they tend to suppress negative emotions or push them away when in the corporate realm. In reality, though, they get hooked on these emotions, creating unhealthy and unsustainable habits to try to control them.

Acceptance of ALL our emotions – even the messy, difficult ones – is the cornerstone to resilience and thriving and true, authentic happiness.

Emotions are the gauges and indicators on the dashboard that give us useful information to make our decisions better.

Emotional agility is a process that allows us to change or maintain our behaviours in ways that align with our intentions and values.

Susan David

Without emotionally healthy people, we cannot have agile organizations.

Jonathan H Westover

Business Agility is impossible if a company's employees are out of touch with their emotions. Susan David (2017) developed the idea of Emotional Agility after studying emotions, happiness, and achievement for more than twenty years. She found that no matter how intelligent or creative people are, or what type of personality they have, how they navigate their inner world—their thoughts, feelings, and self-talk—

ultimately determines how successful they will become. Susan believes engaging with our emotions shapes our actions and how we lead. This challenges the notion that feelings have no place in work. We need to leverage our thoughts and feelings to expect and solve problems and to ensure we do not get stuck. Emotional agility is a radical acceptance of our emotions and learning to respond and not react to them. We can be emotionally rigid or emotionally agile. Emotional agility gives you control over your life and emotions. It is about leaning into your emotions instead of being derailed by them.

Emotional Rigidity	**Emotional Agility**
I am always *reacting* to the pressures of the world around me - chasing my days!	I *decide* how I show up.
I get *stuck* - I am not able to dig myself out of a hole (despair, frustration, boredom).	I am able to *shift* my emotional state so that I can continue stepping forward in my life.
I am letting life pass me by, stagnant in my job and *scared* to step up.	I *choose* courage; ask for a promotion, develop a new skill, take life by the balls.
My emotions make me *uneasy*.	I *lean into* my emotions and try to figure out what they are telling me.

Source: Improvus

Emotional Agility is the ability to approach your inner world flexibly and productively so you can optimally respond even in difficult situations. As humans, we are all prone to common hooks—self-doubt, shame, sadness, fear, or anger—that can too easily steer us in the wrong direction. However, we should not become hooked by our negative feelings – this happens when we treat thoughts and feelings as facts and don't check them out or try to rationalise thoughts and emotions when we know the situation goes against our core values and goals.

Effective leaders, David and Congleton (2013) say, "don't buy into or try to suppress their inner experiences. Instead, they approach them in a mindful, values-driven and productive way – with emotional agility". Some methods can help you unhook from these inner experiences and chatter. You need to notice when you get hooked, then label the thoughts and emotions, accept them and act based on your values and goals.

For example, saying "I'm angry at my co-worker" emphasizes the target of the emotion, but "I feel angry about something my co-worker did" shifts the focus to the emotion and helps to get to the bottom of why that emotion is related to the situation. Similarly, "My work isn't good enough" doesn't identify negative thought patterns like "I have the thought that my work isn't good enough."

https://www.business2community.com/communications/ the-importance-of-emotional-agility-in-the-workplace-02076802

Melissa Anderson writes that it takes an intentional effort to cultivate emotional agility on an organisational level. Leaders must consciously show an adaptable mindset that interprets mistakes as opportunities to cultivate resilience and optimism. While developed organically in some individuals, fostering this trait across an organisation does not happen by accident. By design the workplace supports the development of emotional agility. Allowing emotions in the workplace also promotes great relationships and increased networking.

Emotional agile leaders set the tone for what is appropriate in terms of emotional expression in organisations and display a broad range of emotions in appropriate ways allowing others to do the same. The provide outlets for emotional expression and show empathy and compassion when required. The bottom line is that organisations comprise people and healthy people experience various emotions.

This is even more important in hybrid and remote leadership focusing on burnout and wellness and where people are reporting loneliness, isolation, and disengagement. Leaders need to be emotionally available and aware and show up as human. Satya Nadella, the Microsoft CEO, believes in the power of empathy. The Microsoft leadership framework shows this: Model Coach Care. Let me share an example of a leader enacting this in Microsoft.

Brian Murphy – Senior Director: Employee Skilling Microsoft
Brian believes a leader's key mission is to "create the conditions for people to be at their best". You need a "thriving team" orientation. He leads using these nine principles:

1. Create psychological safety and trust.
2. Lead with vulnerability and curiosity.
3. Coach don't tell.
4. Put yourself in others' shoes.
5. Strive for diversity of views and opinions, including those at odds with your own.
6. Create clarity of purpose and mission.
7. Focus on the conditions needed to realise these.
8. The 'How' of our work is more important than the 'what'.
9. Be the change you want to see in others.

Is This A Gap For You?

Complete Susan David's Emotional Agility Quiz

https://www.susandavid.com/quiz/

Insight

Set Your Goal And Develop Your Immunity To Change Map

Improvement goal	Doing/not doing instead	Hidden competing commitments	Big assumption

RESOURCES

Books

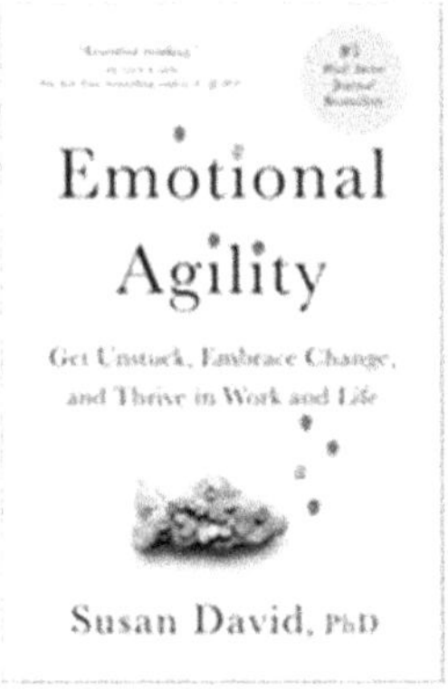
Emotional
Agility
Susan David, PhD

DELIBERATE
CALM
HOW TO LEARN
AND
LEAD IN A
VOLATILE WORLD

Articles

https://hbr.org/2016/11/3-ways-to-better-understand-your-emotions
https://hbr.org/2013/11/emotional-agility

Video Clips And Podcasts

https://www.youtube.com/watch?v=0_6hu6JLH98 Susan David on Emotional Agility 6:55

https://www.ted.com/talks/susan_david_the_gift_and_power_of_emotional_courage?language=en 16:39

https://www.youtube.com/watch?v=nfDVhKP9vak 6 min 4 steps to emotional agility Susan David

https://www.susandavid.com/podcast

PERSONAL AGILITY PRACTICE 5: FOCUS AND DEEP WORK

I build my days around a core of carefully chosen deep work, with the shallow activities I absolutely cannot avoid batched into smaller bursts at the peripheries of my schedule. My goal, of course, is not to make a rigid plan I must follow no matter what. Like most people, my schedule often shifts as the day unfolds. The key, instead, is to make sure that I am intentional about what I do with my time, and don't allow myself to drift along in a haze of reactive,

inbox-driven busyness.

Cal Newport

The idea of Deep Work was coined by Cal Newport, a renowned author and computer science professor at Georgetown University, in a 2012 blog post and expanded upon in his 2016 bestselling book, Deep Work: Rules for Focused Success in a Distracted World. By Newport's definition, Deep Work refers to:

"Professional activity performed in a state of distraction-free concentration that push your cognitive capabilities to their limit. These efforts create new value, improve your skill, and are hard to replicate."

Shallow work is spending our days instead in a frantic blur of e-mail, meetings, and social media. Shallow work is non-cognitively demanding, logistical-style tasks, often performed while distracted. These efforts tend to not create much new value in the world and are easy to replicate.

Many of us have forgotten how to focus deeply on a single task or never really learned to in the first place. Learning how to practice deep work requires you to be more intentional than you've ever been in sitting down regularly to concentrate on high-impact tasks. These strategies will help you select your preferred form of deep work, build a routine from scratch, and provide operating principles and tactics for embracing the power of directed focus.

Distractions are the enemy of deep work. Unfortunately, they're everywhere in the form of your Twitter timeline, Instagram feed, Slack notifications, and email inbox. You can start the day with the best of intentions, an ample to-do list, and a game plan to do everything. Yet, the hours slip, and you fail to accomplish anything meaningful. Newport makes this important point: "efforts to deepen your focus will struggle if you don't simultaneously wean your mind from a dependence on distraction." Newport suggests that "to master the art of deep work… you must take back control of your time and attention from the many diversions that attempt to steal them."

Unfortunately, as valuable as deep work is, it can't be done in unlimited quantity. Newport suggests the upper limit for deep work per day is four hours. Deep work can also be done collaboratively. And remember, deep work is also about prioritising downtime to replenish your concentration.

Other authors write about working smarter and not harder. This includes setting clear boundaries and being intentional about how you spend your time. All great leaders have disciplines they adhere to: Warren Buffett schedules no meeting days so he can think, and Jeff Bezos starts his first meetings at 10 am to give him time to think in the morning.

Newport's own practices include scheduling 4 x 90-minute uninterrupted deep work sessions in my diary each week, using the first 30 min of each day to reflect on my 1-2 key priorities and people I need to contact that day, theming my days, i.e., research day, client day, etc., so I can focus.

Learning how **Vas Narasimhan, CEO of Novartis** manages his energy and not his time is an inspiration for all of us.

"I've found that rather than just managing my time and my calendar, I need to maximize my impact by consciously managing my energy. Like athletes, I have to prepare myself physically and mentally so I can perform at my best. It's the only way I'll have the energy I need as CEO and for the most important titles I hold: dad and husband. If I had to sum up the secret to doing this successfully in one word, I'd say it all comes down to **discipline**. I have been working at this for many years, and I've come up with a series of habits to help ensure I have more energy for Novartis and for my family." Some of his habits include:

- I try to sleep 7 hours every night, and I take 20-minute power naps when traveling and when jet lagged. Consistently, studies show that sleeping has a powerful positive impact on health and on our mental state.
- I do my best to take my weekends off and to not send emails from Friday at 10:00 p.m. until Monday morning unless absolutely critical. I'm aware that any one email I send can lead to 100-500 subsequent emails in the organization.
- I take all of my vacation days (my wife and I love exploring the world with our sons), and I try to fully disconnect during vacation. I check my email only once in the morning and once before bed."

https://www.linkedin.com/pulse/managing-my-energy-time-vas-narasimhan/

Is This A Gap For You?

1. I focus my time well and feel in control of my diary.
2. I keep distractions to a minimum throughout my day.
3. I can give my full attention to thoughts and conversations.
4. I do not multitask.
5. I intentionally schedule deep work and do shallow tasks at the edges of my schedule.

Insight

Set Your Goal And Develop Your Immunity To Change Map

Improvement goal	Doing/not doing instead	Hidden competing commitments	Big assumption

RESOURCES

Books

DEEP
WORK
RULES FOR
FOCUSED
SUCCESS
IN A
DISTRACTED
WORLD
Cal Newport

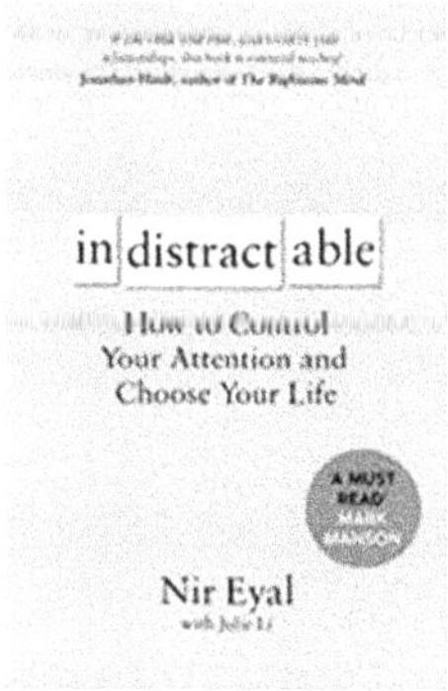
in distract able
How to Control
Your Attention and
Choose Your Life
A MUST READ
Nir Eyal

A
DANIEL GOLEMAN
FOCUS
THE HIDDEN
DRIVER OF
EXCELLENCE
B

Articles

https://hbr.org/2018/03/to-control-your-life-control-what-you-pay-attention-to

https://hbr.org/2018/12/how-timeboxing-works-and-why-it-will-make-you-more-productive

https://hbr.org/2013/12/the-focused-leader

Video Clips And Podcasts

Success in a distracted world: Deep Work by Cal Newport (7:30) https://www.youtube.com/watch?v=1Cn1lZM5LNU Nir Eyal 31 min

https://www.youtube.com/watch?v=Nexy76Jtu24 Daniel Goleman 6:22

CHAPTER 8

The Foundation: Ethical And Moral Maturity

I display ETHICAL AND MORAL MATURITY consistently

The most dangerous obstacles for leaders are personal weakness and self-interest rather than full-scale corruption.

Daft

Ethical Intelligence is the ability of humans to make ethical decisions through principled thinking, choosing, and behaving when faced with moral challenges.

Brent Kedzierski

Until recently, the ethics and morals of leaders have been philosophical. However, with the increasing number of ethical leadership failures and the negative impact this has had, the dimensions of ethics and morality have been proposed to be critical capabilities and mindsets of exemplary leaders (Copeland, 2014). Pressure is mounting to do the right thing, but we have a long way to go. The How Institute found that only 24% of CEOs show virtue, high integrity and commitment to doing the right thing and only 8% of CEOs consistently show moral leadership behaviours which include:

- Living their values and acting on their principles even when uncomfortable or difficult
- Constantly wrestling with questions of right and wrong, fairness and justice and
- Refusing to sacrifice principles for short-term gain.

Cohen, 2023

Ethical leadership does not simply emerge from a code of conduct, a good school, or a host of good intentions. It is an individual choice, or rather choices that emerge from the complex interaction of personal values with social imperatives. The definition of ethical leadership is a state of basing all management decisions, values, and morals on specific principles such as fairness, equality, honesty, respect, and accountability. These values support any ethical leadership.

As a leader, you will be confronted with moral dilemmas in small and big ways. A moral dilemma typically involves a situation in which a difficult decision must be made regarding two or more choices that are not necessarily moral or ethical. There are times when we come across moral dilemmas that test our mental prowess and judgment. We must decide which is the lesser of two evils. Often, there is no easy or correct choice.

What is important to note is that moral decline does not happen in big and unexpected ways. It happens gradually – the first-time people see they can get away with something and it goes unnoticed, the door opens. They then justify their behaviour – "it is not such a big deal", or "everyone is doing it". They then take bigger and bigger risks, and the moral decay sets in.

Here is an example of an organisational ethical dilemma.

> A company's management may aggressively steer its employees and managers towards using a misleading form of accounting. This could be done to greatly inflate the company's profits and mislead market analysts and shareholders. The management can use misleading accounting reports to deceive the public and shareholders about the company's financial performance, which is clearly of personal interest to the management.
>
> But, it is the employees who will face the ethical dilemma as they would be pressurized by their bosses to be involved in unfair and unethical business practices, and refusal to do so might even lead to employees losing their job creating a sense of negativity in the organizational behaviour. This is a situation of ethical dilemma in the organization as employees must choose between keeping their job or being involved in unfair business practices along with the management. This is a situation involving an ethical dilemma as the employees would have to make a tough decision from the viewpoint of their moralities.
>
> https://assignmenthelp4me.com/blog/ethical -dilemmas-in-organizations.html

Ethically intelligent leaders continually grow their competence in questioning, processing, and responding to ethical issues. They practice ethical sensitivity, reasoning, decision-making, reflection, and principle-based care. They use ethical reasoning consistently. (Kedzierski, 2022).

Ethical reasoning is a type of critical thinking that uses ethical principles and frameworks. It is identifying ethical issues and weighing multiple perspectives to make informed decisions. Ethical reasoning is not about knowing right from wrong but thinking about and responding to a problem fairly, justly, and responsibly.

If you do not work on your moral maturity and ethical reasoning skills, you will always struggle to build trust with others. It is your character as a leader on display. Consistent ethics and morals lead to an increase in leadership effectiveness and trust. And it takes courage. Sekerka and Bagozzi (2007) defined moral courage as the ability to use inner principles to do what is good for others, despite a threat to self, as a matter of practice.

The literature suggests that a leader's core values and beliefs are the foundation of their character and are the cognitive structures that influence the leader's awareness of ethical and moral issues, judgement, and behaviour. Moral maturity and ethical judgement are the ability to deal with complex dilemmas that involve competing values.

How much a leader can integrate these values and beliefs into their identity, influences the consistency of their moral and ethical behaviour. Leaders need to work in different situational realities to apply and maintain their values and beliefs effectively.

Ultimately there are different levels of moral development (Kohlberg – see Figure 10). Leaders in the future of work utilise post-conventional vantage points.

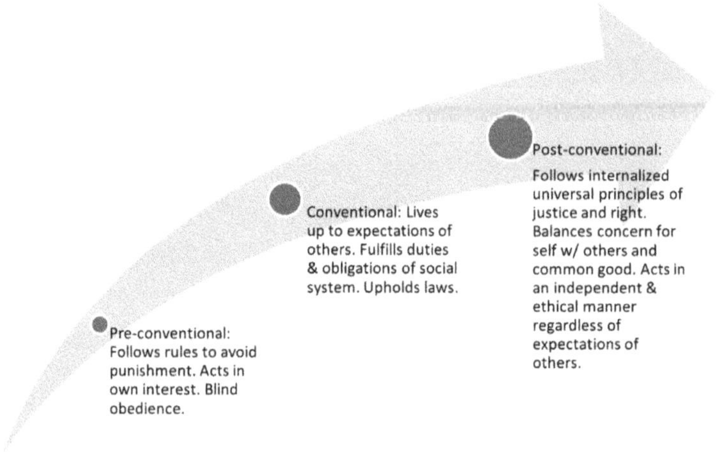
Post-conventional:
Follows internalized universal principles of justice and right. Balances concern for self w/ others and common good. Acts in an independent & ethical manner regardless of expectations of others.
Conventional: Lives up to expectations of others. Fulfills duties & obligations of social system. Upholds laws.
Pre-conventional: Follows rules to avoid punishment. Acts in own interest. Blind obedience.

Figure 10: Kohlberg's stages of moral development

Source: McLeod, 2013

Understand where moral lapses are most probably in business so you can be on the lookout for them. In a recent article by Manfred Hoefle, he calls out these areas where moral lapses are at higher risk: closed, highly competitive groups and cultures, anonymous and depersonalised relationships, excessive incentivisation, pressure on numbers only and huge pay gaps and self-interest being rewarded. Make sure your leaders role model the right behaviours and share stories of moral dilemmas and making the right decisions. Ensure controls are in place and remind people why they are there. Ensure the Board asks the right questions and maintains a culture of psychological safety.

Politically Virtuous

Amy Cohen (2023) calls out being Politically Virtuous as one of the leadership paradoxes leaders must navigate effectively. Power and politics can be difficult to work with - it requires a level of being both politically savvy AND living your values and truths.

CEOs are more likely to be dismissed due to ethical lapses than for poor financial performance or board conflicts. As well as ethical performance, leaders also need political savvy. Positive change is the outcome of successful political maneuvering. So being virtuous and being political have to be intertwined and understanding the social system in the organisation is critical.

Most importantly, leaders need to untangle power and politics. Rather it is about the skill to leverage relationships through networking and influencing positively. There is no running away from this. You need to be willing to engage in politics and have the discipline of staying focused on the purpose and your values.

Moral Courage

Moral courage is the ability to overcome fear to do what is right. It is about taking action when it is not easy. There is no grey area. Every time you stay silent, look on, and do nothing, whilst a morally dubious decision or behaviour goes by, you are setting the precedent and you are complicit. (Cohen, 2023).

Leaders must often find the strength and courage to resist temptations or to stand up for moral principles. Most researchers agree that courage is the ability to step forward through fear and discomfort and take responsibility. It also often means nonconformity and going against the grain. It is not good enough to say, “But I am not the one doing the wrong thing”.

I always recall the great speech made by previous Chief of the Australian Army Lieutenant-General David Morrison, after a sex scandal in the army. His words have been quoted many times. He was visibly shaking with anger as he made his speech.

"The standard you walk past is the standard you accept. If that does not suit you, get out. If you become aware of any individual degrading another, then show moral courage and take a stand against it. Every one of us is responsible for the culture and reputation of our army and the environment in which we work."

Here are some leaders who have taken the high road under very difficult circumstances and stayed true to their purpose and values consistently.

Saks (Sakhiwo) Ntombela – ex-Hollard Group CEO, current Board Director: Coronation Fund Managers

It all starts with being clear about your and the organisation's purpose. My purpose is to *create a caring world that is fair*. And you have to fight hard for purpose because the world is mostly driven by self-interest. You must create a connection for your people to the purpose to use as a frame for decisions they make.

It is critical to combine a low ego with a clear sense of the non-negotiables. And to act on it. One of my biggest regrets as a leader is not acting quicker to move people on that are toxic.

Giam Swiegers – Chairman, Aurecon, Former Group CEO, Aurecon, Former Deloitte Australia CEO

During the global financial crisis, for example, when everyone retrenched heavily, we at Deloitte Australia decided to keep our staff and redirect them. It was 6 months where I slept very little because I was so freaked out about going against the accepted view. But it paid off and it taught me that tough things will happen, and the world goes on.

Is This A Gap For You?

There are 7 elements of moral maturity (Mathieson, 2003). Assess yourself against them:

1. **Moral agency and sense of self** – I can see myself having the right and the ability to make ethical decisions and act on them. I understand and appreciate my responsibility to act for the good.
2. **Harnessing cognitive ability** – when solving a moral dilemma, I identify the stakeholders, evaluate their interest, understand the conflict between principles and make the tradeoffs I need to make. More mature individuals make better use of evidence than others when they judge a situation.
3. **Harness emotional resources** – I understand my emotional response with my rational analysis and how it affects my decisions.
4. **Using Social Skill** – morally mature people know that group norms affect behaviour and understand social pressure. I can maintain my commitment to my principles in the face of group pressure.

5. **Using principles** – I use a clear set of principles when I make decisions.
6. **Respecting others** – I can interact with others who see things differently without feeling that my worldview is threatened.
7. **A sense of purpose** – I understand my service to the world and others.

It is important to note that most people do not reach full moral maturity during their lifetime – it is ongoing work. Identify where you can develop further and start with small actions. Reflect on your insights here.

Insight

Set Your Goal And Develop Your Immunity To Change Map

Improvement goal	Doing/not doing instead	Hidden competing commitments	Big assumption

RESOURCES

Books

ETHICAL
REASONING
THEORY
& APPLICATION
ANDREW
KERNOHAN

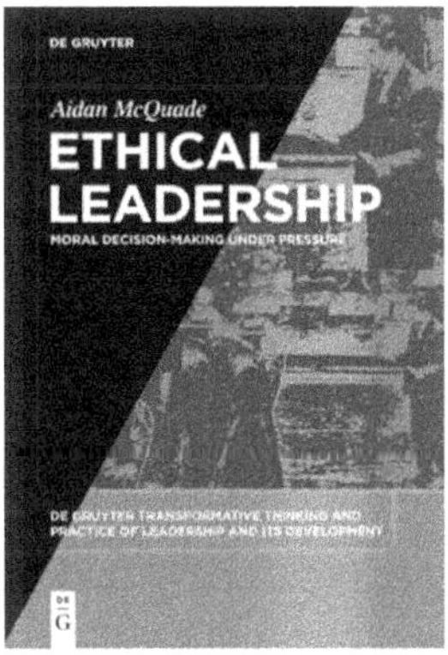
DE GRUYTER
Aidan McQuade
ETHICAL
LEADERSHIP
MORAL DECISION-MAKING UNDER PRESSURE

Articles

https://hbr.org/2021/11/building-an-ethical-company

https://hbr.org/2020/09/a-new-model-for-ethical-leadership

https://hbr.org/1994/03/managing-for-organizational-integrity

Video Clips And Podcasts

https://www.youtube.com/watch?v=145YHrnfeqc 3:11 Stages of moral development

CHAPTER 9

The Vantage Point: Identity

I understand and evolve how I make meaning so I can work in more complexity
IDENTITY

Most developmental psychologists agree that what differentiates leaders is not so much their philosophy of leadership, their personality, or their style of management. Rather, it's their internal "action logic"—how they interpret their surroundings and react when their power or safety is challenged. Relatively few leaders, however, try to understand their own action logic, and fewer still have explored the possibility of changing it.

Rooke & Torbert

Complexity of self is achieved by seeking growth and development, welcoming challenging experiences that stretch one's understanding and equilibrium, exposing oneself to multiple perspectives, seeking and accepting feedback, listening and reflecting and, importantly, taking the risk of acting amidst uncertainty with the best of intentions for the good of the whole system, not just one's own domain.

Ted Billies

Ego represents the striving of human beings to understand themselves and the world they live in. It is the tireless organizer, interpreter, and synthesizer of experience. Ego underlies the universal drive to explain everything and make us feel safe, important, and to belong. People's stage of development influences what they notice and can become aware of, and therefore, what they can describe, articulate, cultivate, influence, and change.

Cooke Greuter

A leader who wants to bring about transformative change within an organisation must possess cognitive capacity one level beyond that which is requisite for their current role—in order "to step outside what is, then plan for and execute the transformation.

Day

Because we don't think of ourselves as changing in the future, we focus our energy on projecting—and protecting—the person we have become, not on growing into the person we might become next. We are caught in the identity mind trap.

Berger & Achi

Is your ego destroying your leadership? According to Garvey Berger and Achi (2020), we are trapped by our own egos, which defines our identity as a leader. Your identity as a leader is connected to your ego action logic.

One's action logic significantly affects how one understands one's role and function in the workplace, how one interacts with other people, and how one deals with adversity and complex issues. One's current action logic also describes how one likely deals with problems. It predicts what one defines as a problem to be solved or simply an unavoidable polarity to be managed. Studies show that the stage of meaning-making is often more powerful in explaining individual differences in behaviour than personality traits and intelligence combined. We constantly seek to manage the impression others have of us, subconsciously defending who we are (which also makes us immune to change).

According to Garvey Berger, common mind traps stop us from evolving. These are:

- We are trapped by simple stories. Our desire for a simple story blind us to a real one.
- We are trapped by rightness. Just because something *feels* right doesn't mean it *is* right.
- We are trapped by agreement. Longing for alignment robs us of good ideas.
- We are trapped by control. Trying to take charge strips us of influence.
- We are trapped by our ego. Shackled to who we are now, we can't reach for who we'll be next.

The good news is we can grow and evolve our ego action logics and unshackle ourselves from our mind traps, although it requires time, self-awareness and examining hidden beliefs that govern our identity. It also requires humility. With moral maturity, we need to become more complex in our assumptions and how we make meaning. This is not an easy task. Our ego is connected to how we show up. It takes time and an intentional approach to slow down, observe more, gather more perspectives, look for connections and patterns, embrace paradoxes and accept other views as equally valid to your own. It also means we become comfortable with challenges we cannot solve through deep expertise or linear, analytical problem-solving. We become adept at understanding when a problem is technical and when it is adaptive and emergent.

According to Ronald Heifetz and his co-authors (2009), the "most common cause of failure in leadership" comes from "treating adaptive challenges as if they were technical problems." To solve adaptive problems which we face more in the future of work context, we need to work from an achiever, individualist, strategist mindset and approach.

We each have a typical way of decision-making and relating to others – the stage we operate from most. HINT: We usually over-estimate our own level. This is our centre-of-gravity action-logic. We call the 7 most common styles of thinking-in-action. They are shown in Figure 11 below.

OPPORTUNIST
Key characteristics
Wins any way possible.
Self orientated
Manipulative
"Might makes right".
DIPLOMAT
Key characteristics
Avoids over conflict
Wants to belong
Obeys group norm
Rarely rocks the boat.
EXPERT
Key characteristics
Rules by logic and expertise
Obeys group norm
Rarely rocks the boat.
ACHIEVER
Key characteristics
Meets strategic goals
Delivery of results by most effective means
Success focused.
INDIVIDUALIST
Key characteristics
Innovates processes
Relativistic position with fewer fixed truths
Self, relationships and interaction with the system.
STRATEGIST
Key characteristics
Creates personal and organizational transformations
Links between principles contracts, theories and judgement.
ALCHEMIST
Key characteristics
Generates social transformations
Interplay of awarenes, thought action and effect
Transforming self and others.

Figure 11: Ego action logics

The Opportunist

The Opportunist Leader is egocentric, untrustworthy, and often displays manipulative behaviour. These leaders are driven only by personal gains, and what they can get from any situation is driven by what they can get to satisfy their needs. They are also known for placing blame on others, even when this is not deserved, to make themselves look better.

Opportunistic leaders are challenging to work for as they see other people as competition and often exploit situations to suit their agenda. Generally, they do not survive long in leadership positions as they can make working life very difficult and unpleasant for others. When you operate from selfishness as modus operandi, your leadership skills will stutter.

The Diplomat

The Diplomatic Leader is one who seeks to please the people around them, especially those who are in more senior positions than they are. They will try to avoid conflict at all costs, which can be problematic if they are in a senior leadership position where inevitable conflict occurs.

Diplomats are mostly polite, sometimes overly so, and friendly, and this means that they struggle to give honest, constructive feedback as they don't want to hurt anyone's feelings or cause any potential situation of tension or conflict. Whilst Diplomats are afraid of conflict, generally, they can perform daily tasks required successfully.

The Expert

The Expert Leader continually seeks more knowledge both at work and outside of work, to be an expert. They will also be a person who seeks to control the environment around them with their knowledge. They try to continuously improve, be efficient and use data and logic to back up their decision-making.

This individual can be challenging to work for as they are generally 'always right' and are not fans of collaboration. They believe their way of doing anything is the best, so what's the need to include anybody else?

Achiever

The Achiever Leader challenges their employees and supports their team whenever needed. They can create a positive and productive work environment successfully and can better work with others than the Expert, the Opportunist, and the Diplomat.

Achievers receive feedback well, see the benefit of influencing those around them positively and can resolve conflicts by being open and compassionate. They can also delegate effectively, plan for both short- and long-term goals and generally have far higher staff retention levels than other leadership styles.

The Individualist

The Individualist Leader recognises that none of the existing action logics are natural. At this stage, leaders can add unique value to an organization due to the realisation that the world is subjectively experienced. They can communicate well and relate to other points of view.

Conversesely, Individualists are prone to not following rules if they deem them useless or irrelevant. This can lead to frustration, tension, and conflict.

For example, it can create incompetent work projects. If the individualist leader thinks there may be a better way to do something, following external instructions can be an issue. Hence, they can be ineffective team players and don't share an organisation's overall vision and mission.

The Strategist

The Strategist Leader will focus on the second-order organisational impact of people's actions and agreements. Because of this, these leaders can create shared visions across different action logics that can work towards organisational transformations.

Within a Strategist leader's action logic, they cope better with conflict than those who exist within other action logics. They are better at dealing with other people's instinctive and emotional reactions, making them resilient and able to drive change.

They continuously seek an idealistic vision with practical and realistic ideas and actions.

The Alchemist

The Alchemist Leaders actions come from the action logic where they can easily and often reinvent themselves within their organisation depending on the situation and circumstances.

These individuals can talk with anyone of any status and can work on both long-term and short-term goals simultaneously with ease.

Alchemist leaders are rare to find in business (and in broader life). They are usually charismatic, personable, likeable, and highly aware.

https://alexhickman.co.uk/the-seven-transformations-of-leadership/

In a complex world, leaders need to operate from an achiever and above action logic. Unfortunately, Opportunists, Diplomats and Experts typically make up about 55% of leaders assessed. About 30% are Achievers and only 15% who consistent capacity to operate at Individualist, Strategist and Alchemist action logics.

To understand just how problematic this is, it is important to know that the first three action logics make up what researchers call the socialised mind – in this form of mind, we mostly protect and project the identity others give us. When others feel good about us, we feel good about ourselves. This has helped us with social glue and shared social frameworks, but it creates the polarities and fault lines we see emerge in society today – where we believe we are right.

Self-authored minds (Achievers, Individualists and Strategists) seek to write their own stories, drawing from an internal operating system of values, beliefs, and a sense of purpose. They still care about what others think, but when they clash with their beliefs, they look at it critically, instead of accepting it. Only 1% of leaders have a self-transforming mind (Alchemist). These individuals believe in not controlling things but in letting things evolve. The focus they take is much larger and longer-term based on larger social and environmental agendas. There is a deep comfort with discomfort and uncertainty.

Our reflex to protect our egos never leaves us, but as we ask ourselves different questions, we can discover—and follow—a development path that enriches us as human beings and ultimately benefits our teams, organizations, and even the world. (Berger and Achi).

One leader that continuously shows up in this book is the Novartis CEO Vas Narasimhan. Let's look at how he managed his ego action logic development. Novartis CEO Vas Narasimhan.

Vas works with Jennifer Garvey Berger to continually develop his ego action logic. He calls himself a "work in progress". Jennifer specializes in Adult Development Theory, which focuses on how we grow and develop as adults. Vas says: "She has pushed me to grow in how I see the world, how I experience my own mind, and how I can use my own growth to power the culture change at Novartis.

I've always been a big believer in the wisdom of the Tao Te Ching and other ancient texts on leadership, but I've seen how Adult Development Theory can be a powerful modern framework for thinking about how to continue developing throughout adulthood, challenging your worldview, and navigating ambiguity and complexity when answers don't come easily. We're adopting this kind of framework at Novartis as we continue transforming our culture and developing our 108,000+ associates around the world—for example, by having hundreds of our people managers participate in extended and personalized leadership development that is aligned with Adult Development Theory."

https://www.linkedin.com/pulse/leaders-never-go-alone-vas-narasimhan

Another leader that continues to expand his level of meaning making is Mteto Nyati, BSG Chairman, Founder Wazo Investments, Former Group CEO, Altron, South Africa. Let's look at what he says below.

"To deal with dynamic complexity, one must understand deeply the connection and interrelatedness between things. Systems thinking is critical for good leadership.

Understand that the answers lie anywhere within your organisation. Be open to be influenced. The practice I used to do is just to connect at different levels of the organisation. Sitting with people closest to the customer – have roundtables with them to understand the issues and symptoms – you can then add this to your understanding of the systems underlying their issues. The insights from the people on the ground are critical. Be open to letting your assumptions be challenged and change your assumptions when required."

Is This A Gap For You?

This is some of the hardest, longest-term work you will need to do as a leader. I recommend you spend one of your learning sprints every year focusing back on your ego action logic. Look at each level's descriptions and assess where you think you are most comfortable. Ask others what they think. Also think about what you revert to under pressure. This is not an exact measure but a starting point to reflect on.

Action Logic	Description	How I show up
Opportunist	Focus on personal wins and see the world and other people as opportunities to be exploited. Wants to be in control and manipulates others.	
Diplomat	Focuses on pleasing higher-status colleagues and avoids conflict – whilst this is helpful at more junior levels of leadership, it becomes problematic at senior levels. Senior leaders need to be good at conflict. Diplomats are over polite, and they struggle to give others feedback.	
Expert	This is the largest category leaders fall into and the most important to shift. Rules by logic and expertise and seeks rational efficiency. Focused on process, knowledge, and experience. Wants to get everything perfect. Good as an individual contributor but struggles to lead and collaborate.	

Achievers	Open to feedback and learning. Focus on deliverables and creating functioning teams but is not good yet at thinking out of the box and challenging the status quo. Often clash with Experts.	
Individualist	Can work well with all other action logics, does not take things personally and listens to and considers all views, taking a broad and systemic perspective. Uses principles and values to make decisions and are willing to challenge the status quo.	

Action Logic	**Description**	**How I show up**
Strategist	Great at understanding the impact of decisions and transforming culture and performance over the long term – can manage resistance to change and harness conflict well – understands the interplay between the organisation and its context and focuses on creating ethical, sustainable organisations.	
Alchemist	Can renew and reinvent themselves and their organisations in historically significant ways – usually not in business, but working on larger long-term societal issues.	

Reflect on your insights here.

Insight

Set Your Goal And Develop Your Immunity To Change Map

Improvement goal	Doing/not doing instead	Hidden competing commitments	Big assumption

RESOURCES

Books

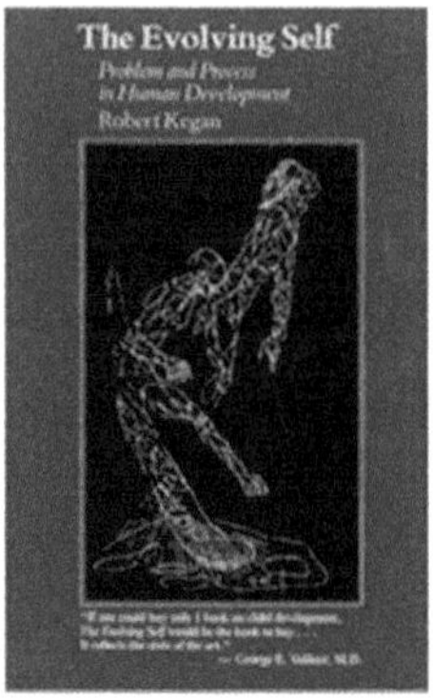
The Evolving Self
Robert Kegan

UNLOCKING
HOW TO THRIVE
LEADERSHIP
IN COMPLEXITY
MINDTRAPS
Jennifer Garvey Berger

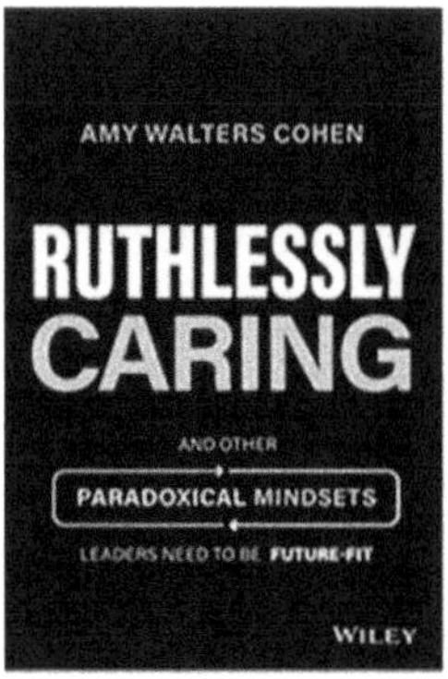
AMY WALTERS COHEN
RUTHLESSLY
CARING
AND OTHER
PARADOXICAL MINDSETS
LEADERS NEED TO BE FUTURE-FIT
WILEY

Articles

https://hbr.org/2005/04/seven-transformations-of-leadership

https://zampellagroup.com/wp-content/uploads/Torbert_Action_Logics.pdf

https://hbr.org/2007/11/a-leaders-framework-for-decision-making

Video Clips And Podcasts

https://www.youtube.com/watch?v=ThzngWNgRIQ_ 22 min Rooke Leadership Transformation

CHAPTER 10

The Game Changer: Collaborative Behaviours

I learn to co-create
and collaborate and
share leadership
COLLABORATIVE
BEHAVIOURS

Most often successful, achievement-oriented people mistakenly believe they are the principal source of accomplishments in their teams and organisations.

Relationships are the bridges that connect authenticity to influence and value creation. Leadership always operates in the context of relationships.

Kevin Cashman

Collaborative leadership is an increasingly vital source of competitive advantage in today's highly networked, team-based, and partnership-oriented business environments. Yet few leaders have been trained to lead collaboratively, especially those at more senior levels who climbed the organisational ladder in a different era.

By collaborative leadership, we mean the process of engaging collective intelligence to deliver results across organisational boundaries when ordinary mechanisms of control are absent. It's grounded in

a belief that all of us together can be smarter, more creative, and more competent than any of us alone, especially when it comes to addressing the kinds of novel, complex, and multi-faceted problems that organisations face today. It calls on leaders to use the power of influence rather than positional authority to engage and align people, focus their teams, sustain momentum, and perform. Success depends on creating an environment of trust, mutual respect, and shared aspiration in which all can contribute fully and openly to achieving collective goals. Leaders must thus focus on relationships as well as results, and the medium through which they operate is high-quality conversation.

Oxford Leadership

High-performing managers stand out from their peers in their ability to tap large, diversified networks that are rich in experience and span organisational boundaries

Cross, Davenport, and Cantrell

Given that the demands many leaders face today are beyond the limits of any one individual's capacity, one of the most important qualities is an interest in collaboration, leveraging shared efforts and group processes.

Ted Billies

When people try to collaborate on everything, they can wind up in endless meetings, debating ideas and struggling to find consensus.

Ibarra and Hansen

As leaders, we're often conditioned to take a zero-sum approach. The more services or products we sell to customers the less our competitors do, and vice versa. The problem with that mindset is that it limits the opportunities to respond quickly, align with those who have complementary resources, and swiftly innovate to deliver to the market efficiently and effectively. Leaders are about networks, not hierarchy. It is about partnerships, eco system and creating belonging and connection.

The World Economic Forum writes that going it alone as an organisation will not work in the complex, ever changing environment we are in. They urge us to transform our business models and prioritise collaboration. Here is a great example.

Mercedes-Benz and BMW who pooled their carsharing services, combined taxi apps and e-scooter providers and created the mobility app FreeNow. The result was a bigger slice of the pie for everyone. These alliances give companies rapid access to technology, skills, and data. A recent EY survey of business leaders operating within at least one ecosystem attribute on average 13.7% of total annual revenues, 12.9% in cost reduction and 13.3% in incremental earnings to working in this way.

https://www.weforum.org/agenda/2023/01/ competition-vs-collaboration-ey-innovation-wef23/

Today the most promising innovation and business opportunities require **collaboration among functions, offices and between organisations.** The best solutions require horizontal collaboration and integration. Harvard's Heidi Gardner has found that firms with more cross-boundary collaboration achieve greater customer loyalty and higher margins. Now, we can redesign the organisation, and to some extent it is important to do so, but that has its limits because it can be costly, confusing, and slow and it does not change silo behaviours.

There are two levels of collaboration. The first, **collaboration across organisational boundaries** requires a management practice that aims to bring managers, executives, and staff out of silos to work together. In collaborative workplaces, information is shared organically, and everyone takes responsibility for the whole. It sits in contrast to traditional top-down organisational models where a small group of executives control the flow of information.

Collaborative leaders, according to Harvard Business Review, regularly seek a diversity of opinions and ideas among teammates to build strategies and solve problems. Employees are more engaged, feel trusted and are more likely to take ownership of their work. Through collaborative leadership, managers and executives can create an inclusive environment that energises teams, releases creativity, and cultivates a work culture that is both productive and joyful.

The problem is that traditionally, managers learn to manage vertically — to work upward with senior colleagues and downward with direct reports. Horizontal boundaries seem to pose the greatest challenge and shows up often in low 360 ratings from peers. The greatest bottleneck seems at middle management, where leaders fail to make a shift to a cross-functional, cross-group mindset.

Collaborative leadership is achieved through strong relationships and crucial conversations. In these conversations, leaders with collaborative behaviour forge a shared purpose and collective goals for the group collaborating, they clarify how the group will engage, who plays which roles and how decisions will be made. But most of all, they ensure that they harness the collective intelligence and diverse perspectives everyone brings.

Collaborative leaders build relationships, networking and showing a genuine interest in others. Ultimately, they engage in complex problem-solving with others. They do not drive a culture of over collaboration and surface-level collaboration. They are intentional and transparent though about their collaboration. They do not invite everyone to every meeting and project and copy everyone into every email.

Leaders with strong, trusting, and authentic relationships with their teams know that investing time in building these bonds makes them more effective as a leader and creates a foundation for success. Leaders are discovering they must proactively invest in the ecosystem and build partnerships (turn vendors into partners; join with competitors to solve problems government can't) to create the conditions for sustainable success.

Then there is **external collaboration and networks**. Did you know that 3% of people in organisations influence all the rest when we conduct organisational network analyses (according to LinkedIn). Are you one of them? We call these people **Super Connectors**. Super-connectors are very selective with their time and intentional about who they spend it with, they discover who gatekeepers are to critical people they want to meet and create relationships with them, they are generous with their time and help with those they choose to connect with, and they expect nothing in return.

Ibarra and Hunter(2007) describe three types of networks you need to build and maintain as a leader – operational, personal, and strategic. You will see these in the table below. The problem is most leaders only focus on operational and personal networks and do not build strategic networks. Of work, that will be a real challenge for leaders operating in effective ecosystems.

THE THREE FORMS OF NETWORKING

Managers who think they are adept at networking are often operating only at an operational or personal level. Effective leaders learn to employ networks for strategic purposes.

	Operational	Personal	Strategic
Purpose	Getting work done efficiently; maintaining the capacities and functions required of the group.	Enhancing personal and professional development; providing referrals to useful information and contacts.	Figuring out future priorities and challenges; getting stakeholder support for them.
Location and temporal orientation	Contacts are mostly internal and oriented toward current demands.	Contacts are mostly external and oriented toward current interests and future potential interests.	Contacts are internal and external and oriented toward the future.
Players and recruitment	Key contacts are relatively nondiscretionary; they are prescribed mostly by the task and organizational structure, so it is very clear who is relevant.	Key contacts are mostly discretionary; it is not always clear who is relevant.	Key contacts follow from the strategic context and the organizational environment, but specific membership is discretionary; it is not always clear who is relevant.
Network attributes and key behaviors	Depth: building strong working relationships.	Breadth: reaching out to contacts who can make referrals.	Leverage: creating inside-outside links.

You also need diverse networks. Ibarra and Hansen (2015) write about a groundbreaking US study of S&P 1500 CEOs which managed to condense leaders' professional networks of business contacts into a single diversity index – a quantifiable value that weighted things like the gender and nationality, education, professional expertise, and global work experience of the CEOs' networks. These networks were contacts those leaders had proactively forged through school or university ties, work ties and social connections.

When the researchers compared network diversity values and looked for ties to the performance and value of the firms in their study, they found that CEOs with more diverse networks create more firm value—because they are more innovative, as measured by patents, and engage in more productive, diversified mergers and acquisition activity. CEOs who were diversely connected (at the 75th percentile of the researcher's "diversity index," as based on gender, nationality, academic degrees, professional expertise, extracurricular activity, and global work experience), compared with those who were simply average, improved Tobin's Q, a ratio of market to book value of assets, at a level equivalent to an $81 million increase in market capitalisation for a median-size firm in their sample.

I have several Professional Services clients, and what they have found is that they now require in the words of Heidi Gardner "Hyper Collaboration" to remain competitive. Their clients' challenges have become more integrated and complex, and to address this, they need to increasingly leverage expertise across the boundaries of their enterprise and practice groups (silo's). That presents a great opportunity. Heidi found in her research that as more practice groups collaborate to serve a client, the average annual revenue from the client increases, over and above what each practice would have earned from selling discrete services separately.

EY has over the last 5 years developed an ecosystem of over 100 alliance partners, including Dell Technologies, IBM, Microsoft, SAP and ServiceNow to benefit EY clients who can unlock sustainable, long-term value due to the data, relationships and technology that these ecosystems offer. EY has also created Neuro-Diverse Centers of Excellence. These operate as an ecosystem of different institutions, where year on year EY and SAP work together to focus business clients, academic institutions, the public sector, and NGOs on applying the talents of individuals with cognitive differences such as dyslexia, ADHD, autism and Asperger's syndrome. This ecosystem's common goal benefits everybody — providing access to diverse skillsets, new ways of thinking and inclusive employment — which wouldn't be possible without collaboration.

Seeing an opportunity to serve an unmet market need, and integrating the contributions of multiple organizations, large and small, to aggregate their capabilities to meet that need, is the magic of an ecosystem. To collaborate effectively across ecosystem boundaries, participants must understand the value they are contributing to the collective opportunity. Ground rules must exist about how conflict will get resolved, where final decision rights lie, and what capabilities the participants must co-create to deliver. If there are gaps in those capabilities, there must be honest conversation about how those gaps will be closed, what investments will be required to close them, and by whom. And the role of trust must be openly discussed – how it will be sustained, how relationships across boundaries will be nurtured and strengthened, and what will be a breach of trust. This is especially important given confidentiality, NDA, and other forms of agreement in which participants protect their respective organizations' competitive secrets while creating mutual market benefit with others for a shared customer.

https://www.forbes.com/sites/roncarucci/2019/10/21/how-collaboration-and-purpose-are-fueling-the-growth-of-market-ecosystems/

It starts with your ability to create and maintain networks and relationships.

Too many leaders see networking and spending time on building relationships as a distraction. Leadership is a social process. It is an ever-changing network of relationships through which leadership is operationalized. Understanding and leveraging your network can help you expand your influence and impact. More is not better. Questions leaders may wish to consider as they refine their network include:

- Which relationships are most critical to achieving my business and career goals?
- How can I establish or maintain these relationships?
- Does my network include diverse points of view?
- Do I have too few relationships in an area (e.g., too few connections outside of my organization)?
- Are all the relationships I'm maintaining genuinely important?

https://contemporaryleadership.com/wp-content/uploads/2021/10/Network-Leadership.pdf

Saks (Sakhiwo) Ntombela – ex-Hollard Group CEO, current Board Director: Coronation Fund Managers

You must connect strongly with people. Whenever I join a new organisation, I set up "chat with Saks sessions" to share who I am, what we should achieve together, how I work and what I expect from people – Integrity, Customer centricity and Getting things done. I let everyone share the same with me. It sets the tone and creates psychological safety. I make sure the teams I lead work well together – I use an 18-month process where we go through personal mastery sessions together. We look at our own and others' lifelines, get to know each other and have clear conversations. Six months later we then work together further on learning how to manage organisations and change and lead the organisation. This leads to trust, the ability to debate issues and shared accountability. I also like having monthly dinners with my team hosted at different people's homes.

To support collaborative behaviours you need to get the incentives right. At Hollard, we measured financial AND social impact and looked at Customer, People and Transformation KPIs. We generated a pool from our profit that could be shared. The EXCO was rewarded based on Group Performance, not individual performance.

Mteto Nyati, BSG Chairman, Founder Wazo Investments, Former Group CEO, Altron, South Africa

We are not an island – we are connected to others. You must understand you are part of an ecosystem. You must positively affect the people in your ecosystem – be intentional about this. Understand their challenges and how you can help, work with them, deepen the relationships – in the process you are also improving your own competitiveness.

Is This A Gap For You?

Complete the assessment in the link below. https://www.surveygizmo.com/s3/5450481/ **Collaboration-Assessment**

Assess the value of your networks. https://hbr.org/2012/06/assess-the-value-of-your-network Reflect on your insights here.

Insight

Set Your Goal And Develop Your Immunity To Change Map

Improvement goal	Doing/not doing instead	Hidden competing commitments	Big assumption

RESOURCES

Books

SMART
COLLABORATION
HEIDI K. GARDNER

The Silo Effect
Why Every Organisation Needs to Disrupt Itself to Survive
Gillian Tett

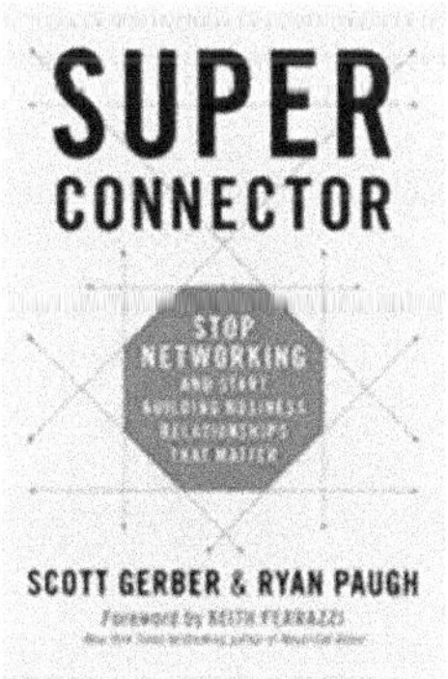
SUPER
CONNECTOR
STOP NETWORKING
SCOTT GERBER & RYAN PAUGH

Articles

https://hbr.org/2011/07/are-you-a-collaborative-leader

https://www.mckinsey.com/capabilities/people-and-organizational-performance/our-insights/making-collaboration-across-functions-a-reality

https://hbr.org/2019/05/cross-silo-leadership

https://hbr.org/2007/11/eight-ways-to-build-collaborative-teams

https://hbr.org/2007/01/how-leaders-create-and-use-networks

Video Clips And Podcasts

https://www.youtube.com/watch?v=1GREuScFAQc
Collaborative Leadership Zenger and Folkman 42 min

https://www.youtube.com/watch?v=hc68qSppJio The Four Stages of Psychological Safety Tom Clark 33 min

CHAPTER 11

Extra Sauce: Updated Future-Fit Competencies

I keep my knowledge and skills relevant
FUTURE FIT COMPETENCIES

Leaders still need to update their knowledge and skills. The obvious ones are skills and knowledge like Industry, Business and Financial knowledge, but there are others that are critical to the future of work context. What differs from previous uses of competencies is this needs to be enacted. It cannot just be another course you thought interesting and file it away. You need to learn and then go and observe and try things out. The learning only happens when we apply it. Our knowledge retention is not very good.

Here are some of the things leaders need to know, not as experts, but have a great understanding of it and be able to think about how it helps the organisation and its people remain competitive and, even better, become a sustainable anti-fragile organisation. Technology, Data and Cyber Security is not IT's problem – you need to have a high-level understanding of it. Human Centred Design is not the Marketing department's problem – as a leader, you need to understand client and employee centred design and experiences. People management and culture is not HR's problem. As a leader, you should understand and manage the cultural narrative and hold yourself and other leaders accountable for leading people. There are many more, and you must understand which matters in your industry. Here are just some ideas of the critical few I come across often as gaps in leadership knowledge and skills and ways to start your development journey.

- Technology, data, and cyber security literacy.
- Complex problem finding and solving (critical thinking).
- Agile methods for delivery and performance.
- Human centred design.
- Human/machine optimisation and the skills-based approach.
- Storytelling.

The best way to continually update your knowledge and skill is to read and do small online courses, learn from others in the organisation and move across areas of expertise in your career. The micro-learning courses are often free or low cost. Once you understand the concepts, talk to others about them and try them out. Micro-credentials are the way to go here, and experience beats all else in learning. The idea is NOT to develop these all at once. Prioritise and learn a bit every year.

FUTURE SKILL 1:

TECHNOLOGY, DIGITAL AND CYBER SECURITY LITERACY

The ability to adapt to novel situations is still a challenge for AI and robotics and a key reason why companies continue to rely on human workers for a variety of tasks.

Autor, Mindell, and Reynolds

Coding is not a leadership skill requirement, but technology literacy is. Avolio et al. (2014) argue that leaders and technology should co-evolve, with leadership being a corporate social structure created by technology. To succeed in the digital age, executives should have about 30 percent fluency in key technologies and technical skills. (Shinn, 2022). Being tech-savvy means understanding concepts like automation, data science, cybersecurity, cloud, information architecture, and data storage, it will mean understanding the tools and platforms for people to work with, etc.

AI, Blockchain and Automation are focuses right now. "AI" has become a catchall term to describe any advancements in computing, systems and technology in which computer programs can perform tasks or solve problems that require the reason we associate with human intelligence, even learning from past processes.

ChatGPT has shaken things up – suddenly, we have a tool that has exceptional writing ability, is proficient at complex tasks and is easy to use. What is ChatGPT? ChatGPT is a prototype dialogue-based AI chatbot capable of understanding natural human language and generating impressively detailed human-like written text. It is the latest evolution of the GPT – or Generative Pre-Trained Transformer – family of text-generating AIs. There has been speculation that professions dependent upon content production could be rendered obsolete, including everything from playwrights and professors to programmers and journalists. I do not think it will replace humans, but the work humans do will evolve and it is your job as a leader to understand this and ensure people are reskilled and jobs are redefined in time. We will be able to do things we could never do before, but only if we are prepared for it. And we better be prepared for the ethical reasoning we will need!

https://www.theguardian.com/technology/2022/dec/05/what-is-ai-chatbot-phenomenon-chatgpt-and-could-it-replace-humans

Another key focus is data literacy. Leaders need to be proficient in data-driven decision-making to drive business impact. Gartner defines data literacy as the ability to read, write and communicate data in context, including an understanding of data sources and constructs, analytical methods and techniques applied, and the ability to describe the use case, application and resulting value. Data-literate leaders:

- Know how to work with data, how it is stored and shared, and how to derive meaning from it.
- Understand the contextual use of data within their domain – how actionable insights can be drawn from data to shape delivery.
- Are data storytellers. They can shape and communicate a narrative about the importance of data in the overarching strategy of their organisation – about how the data they capture leads to actionable insights, which inform data-driven decision-making, which leads directly to positive impacts and outcomes.

https://blog.scottlogic.com/2023/01/12/how-data-literacy-gives-leaders-the-edge.html

They understand cyber security risks as this is the major threat to your organisation. Attacks rose 600% during the pandemic as hackers capitalized on people working from home, on less secure technological systems and Wi-Fi networks. As leaders, we all need to be conscious of the major sources of cybersecurity risk and work with our teams to ensure they understand their role in mitigating those risks. AI and machine learning will be critical tools in identifying and predicting threats in cybersecurity. AI will also be a crucial asset for security in finance, given it can process large amounts of data to predict and catch instances of fraud.

https://www.forbes.com/sites/ashleystahl/2021/03/10/ how-ai-will-impact-the-future-of-work-and-life/

Organisations touted as having deployed successful digital transformations include Nordstrom, IKEA, Lego, Autodesk, Burberry, and Unilever. Nordstrom, for example, has always been known for its elegant, upscale customer experience. When they developed a digital business model and strategy, they wanted to provide the ultimate customer experience. Following the creation of their website, they developed a new point-of-sale system featuring personal book software, so sales could track individual customer requests and needs. The launch of an innovation lab soon followed that enabled the development of social apps, mobile checkout, employee texting, and later, the acquisition of a cloud-based men's personalized clothing service.

https://digitalmarketinginstitute.com/blog/digital-leadership-6-examples-of-brands-that-reign-supreme

Is this a gap for you?

Assess your digital literacy.

https://europa.eu/europass/digitalskills/screen/home

RESOURCES

Books

BEYOND
DIGITAL
How Great Leaders
Transform Their Organizations
and Shape the Future
Paul Leinwand
Mahadeva Matt Mani

"A RIVETING READ."
NO SAFE
HARBOR
THE INSIDE TRUTH
ABOUT CYBERCRIME—
AND HOW TO PROTECT
YOUR BUSINESS
MARK SANGSTER

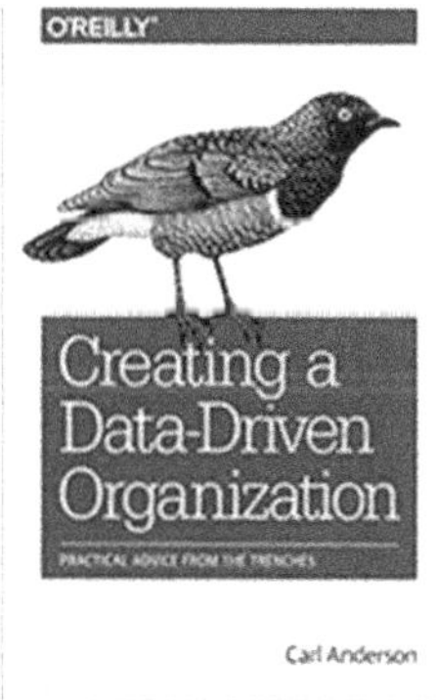
O'REILLY
Creating a
Data-Driven
Organization
PRACTICAL ADVICE FROM THE TRENCHES
Carl Anderson

Articles

https://www.linkedin.com/pulse/how-become-digitally-savvy-leader-marko-luhtala/?trk=public_profile_article_view

https://www.linkedin.com/pulse/

tech-savvy-leader-necessary-leadership-skill-hybrid-world-schubert/

https://www.mckinsey.com/~/media/mckinsey/email/leadingoff/2022/10/03/2022-10-03b.html

https://hbr.org/2022/02/why-becoming-a-data-driven-organization-is-so-hard

https://hbr.org/2020/02/10-steps-to-creating-a-data-driven-culture

https://www.forbes.com/sites/forbesbusinesscouncil/2022/05/19/why-cybersecurity-is-now-a-board-level-leadership-imperative/?sh=86817b74270e

Videos And Podcasts

https://www.youtube.com/watch?v=AUDZP_rCou8 7:42

https://www.ey.com/en_gl/ceo/thriving-in-the-digital-era-at-honeywell 14 min

https://www.youtube.com/watch?v=QWQqxwWhBwA What is ChatGPT and why it is even more massive than you think, Josh Bersin, 18 min

https://www.youtube.com/watch?v=aZmr1kbjwM8 What companies must know about cyber threats and security 15:41

Courses

MIT course on AI leadership

https://executive.mit.edu/course/ai-leadership/054v00000jiN84AAE.html

EdX course on Data Literacy

https://www.edx.org/course/data-literacy-foundations?index=product&queryID=7f74b42226c5ea0dc1ebc79ceec52a43&position=2

Harvard course on Cybersecurity risk management

https://harvardx-onlinecourses.getsmarter.com/presentations/lp/harvard-cybersecurity-online-short-course

FUTURE SKILL 2:

COMPLEX PROBLEM FINDING AND SOLVING (CRITICAL THINKING)

The essence of adopting a problem-finding mindset is a willingness to question the status quo and more importantly, not to be afraid to truly think about the concept of ambiguity itself.

June Kang

If I were given one hour to save the planet, I would spend 59 minutes defining the problem and one minute resolving it.

Albert Einstein

We love a quick fix, but… Are you solving the right problem? And are you solving that problem, right? The nature of problems in the future of work – they are messy, co-produced and wicked. (Fergusson, 2019).

Leaders in the future of work need to work with systemic, wicked, and adaptive problems and dilemmas comfortably. A systemic problem is a system of interrelated problems. It is a "mess". Instead of intervening in one part of the "mess" to improve it, the ideal design school proposes an ideal redesign of the whole mess. Hence, we talk about problem (dis) solving not problem solving. The logic of the solution is not the logic of the problem.

Grint (2008) defines a wicked problem: "A Wicked Problem is more complex, rather than just complicated – that is, it cannot be removed from its environment, solved, and returned without affecting the environment. Moreover, there is no clear relationship between cause and effect." (p.12). He says: The leader's role with a Wicked Problem…is to ask the right questions rather than provide the right answers because the answers may not be self-evident and will require a collaborative process to make any progress. (p.13).

Bob Johansen (2017) writes that leaders of the future will be good at dilemma-flipping – the ability to turn dilemmas into opportunities and advantages. Leaders in the new world can hold opposing ideas in mind comfortably. Dilemma flipping then starts with a mind reset. It means the leader must be able to sense, frame, and then reframe a situation. Reframing means stepping back, checking assumptions and understanding what is and could be going on. One thing leaders need to reframe is being comfortable with paradox.

According to PwC, a paradox involves "contradictory-yet-interrelated elements that exist simultaneously and persist over time."

The six paradoxes are:

1. **Globally minded localist.** Be both deeply embedded in the local market and seamlessly connected across the globe at the same time.
2. **Strategic executor.** Be strategic, solve today's problems with tomorrow in mind, and execute effectively.
3. **High-integrity politician.** Navigate the politics of driving change in your organisation without losing your integrity and character.
4. **Tech-savvy humanist.** Be able to drive technological advancements without sacrificing your focus on your people.
5. **Humble hero.** Act confidently and competently in a VUCA (volatile, uncertain, complex, and ambiguous) environment with

the humility to recognise when you need help and when you are wrong.

6. **Traditioned innovator.** Have the ability to respect and learn from the past and use it to propel the organisation and your team forward into the future, all while creating a culture that does not fear failure but cultivates learning and growth.

https://www.linkedin.com/pulse/getting-comfortable-uncomfortable-paradoxes-leadership-alicia-lykos/?trk=articles_directory

When we step back, we can use our pattern intelligence. We need to look for patterns, not problems. We need to value questions, not answers. We need to embrace ambiguity and nuance vs looking for certainty. And we need to seek coherence, not alignment.

Is this a gap for you?

Assess Yourself

- Do you actively distinguish between tame and wicked problems and adapt your approach?
- Do you seek and evaluate different information, perspectives, and evidence to make sense of the wicked problem?
- Do you try to connect the ideas, information, perspectives, and evidence to understand emerging patterns?
- Do you actively develop ideal future solutions with others to the emerging patterns?
- Do you build roadmaps to start the solutions?

RESOURCES

Books

THE
SYSTEMS
THINKER

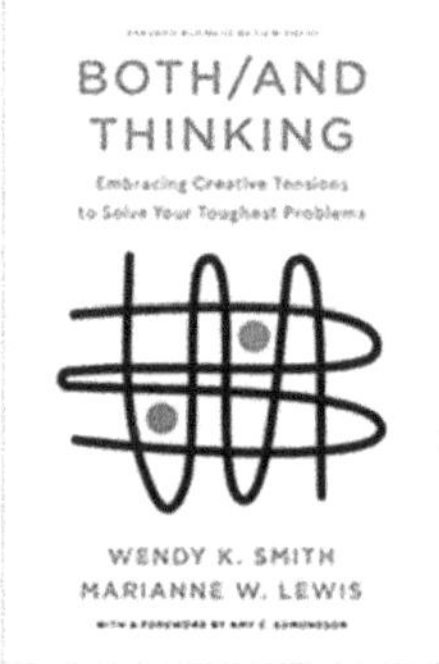
BOTH/AND
THINKING
WENDY K. SMITH
MARIANNE W. LEWIS

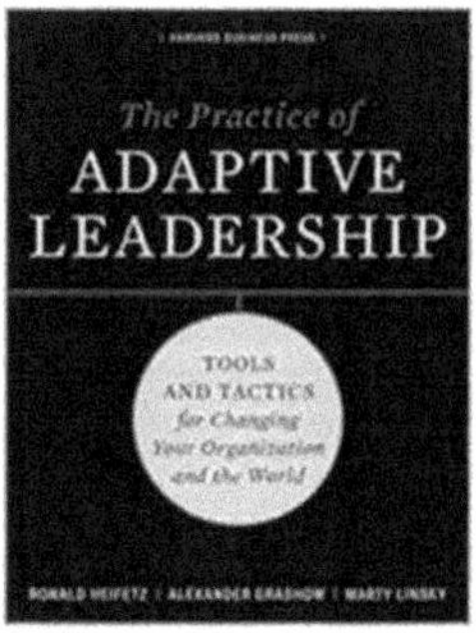
The Practice of
ADAPTIVE
LEADERSHIP

Articles

https://hbr.org/2012/09/are-you-solving-the-right-problem

https://www.pwc.com/gx/en/issues/assets/pdf/six-paradoxes_brochure.pdf

FUTURE SKILL 3:

HUMAN CENTRED DESIGN

People ignore designs that ignore people.

Frank Chimero

A design mindset is action-oriented and solution-focused.

When properly adopted, it helps a leader to become effective, innovative, and transformative.

Roy Prasad

The shake-up felt by the pandemic has taught us a key lesson – organisations must be adaptable to prepare for and overcome periods of instability. Being adaptable means living in a constant stage of change and experimentation…and being comfortable with it. It means showing up with an open, questioning mind.

The magic of design thinking is its human-centric core. Design thinking is inherently participatory and relies on the diversity of thought and perspectives to drive ideas forward. Engaging with stakeholders every step of the way makes sure the design process and ensuing solutions are made with people, for people. This is crucial for future work strategies, where people are actively invested in co-creating their new normal. Using inclusive design methods shows leadership is listening and driven to develop informed policies employees resonate with.

Design thinking is also about collaboration. It uses the power of the collective brain. It means leaders drop their ego and listen to their people and customers. And it drives innovation based on customer and employee needs.

The **Aurecon Group**, an international design, engineering and advisory firm, continually innovate using design thinking to bring ideas to life. They have their own Aurecon Design Academy. Established in 2017, Aurecon Design Academy is their accelerator learning program for technical mastery and design excellence. Formalised by RMIT University into a Graduate Certificate in Design Management, Aurecon Design Academy aims to foster eminence and a human-centred, transdisciplinary approach to design problems, enabling the organisation to serve clients through design excellence and innovation. The organisation's Design Directors are the custodians of the quality of their design and hold a position of authority and responsibility regarding the merit of their design be it bridges, tunnels, water, complex structures, bulk materials, community engagement.

On their website, they say:

At Aurecon, we work and think as designers. Approaching our clients' problems with this mindset ensures we build understanding before we build solutions. It's a considered way of combining our creativity and expertise to move from concept to real outcomes and existing situations to preferred ones by putting people at the centre of the solution. The results are solutions that address the right problem and are designed to put our people and planet first.

https://www.aurecongroup.com/about/future-ready/innovation

Is this a gap for you?

Assess Yourself

- Do you understand design thinking?
- Do you use design thinking?
- Do you understand customer-informed service design?
- Do you understand employee experience design?

RESOURCES

Books

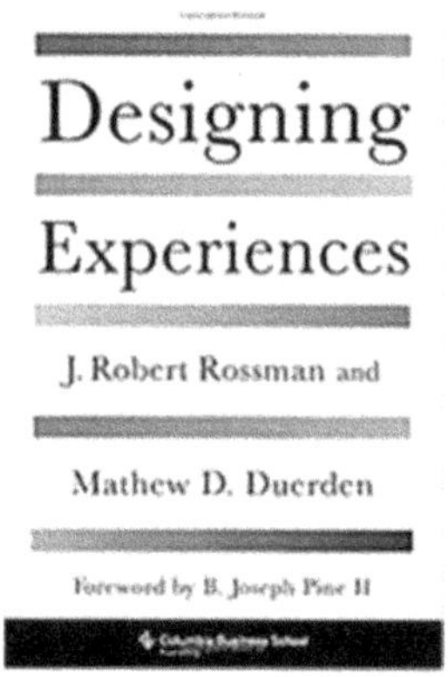
Designing
Experiences
J. Robert Rossman and
Mathew D. Duerden
Foreword by B. Joseph Pine II

BEN WHITTER
2nd edition
EMPLOYEE
EXPERIENCE
Develop a happy, productive and supported workforce for exceptional individual and business performance

Articles

https://www.bcg.com/publications/2020/the-importance-of-human-centered-design

https://businesschief.eu/leadership-and-strategy/

future-of-work-why-a-human-centred-approach-is-key

https://hbr.org/2019/03/the-right-way-to-lead-design-thinking

Videos And Podcasts

https://www.youtube.com/watch?v=WHo3QknArCc 7:27

https://www.youtube.com/watch?v=dcUf2-JvymI Exploration through design at Aurecon, 32 min

FUTURE SKILL 4:

AGILE METHODS FOR DELIVERY AND PERFORMANCE

With agile, leadership shifts from directing to coaching, from telling to empowering and from establishing limits to eliminating roadblocks. Agile leaders get out of the way, checking in on teams rather than checking up, and trusting members to work through problems with little direction. They also encourage risk taking, reassuring teams that experimentation is expected and reinforcing that learning through failure is a positive contribution.

https://www.steelcase.com/research/articles/topics/design/agile-working-new-ways/

Maybe you call it agile, maybe you call in new ways of working. Whatever you call it … is an attitude, not a technique with boundaries. An attitude has no boundaries, so we wouldn't ask "can I use agile here", but rather "how would I act in the agile way here?" or "how agile can we be, here?" Alistair Cockburn (in Andrea Benton (2023)

Large teams aren't as agile as a network of small teams that can be disbanded and reassembled as teams move onto new projects and challenges. The structure focuses on work and projects as teams are more product, customer and service based. This model could work to help bridge the gap between productivity and technology, but to form teams quickly requires clearly understanding everyone's skillset, scorecard, and purpose.

Teams choose agile so they can respond to changes or feedback from customers quickly without derailing a year's worth of plans. "Just enough" planning and shipping in small, frequent increments lets your team gather feedback on each change and integrate it into future at a minimal cost. It is all about a mindset of continuous improvement.

Work is becoming more project-based and cross functional. Work and goals need to be broken into phases and sprints delivered by cross-functional teams. In a world constantly changing. Different tools are used to create momentum and flexibility, including Scrum sprints and daily stand-up meetings (in person or virtual), Kanban boards, Agile project management, Agile at scale and others.

An organisation achieving success with agile at scale is Cisco. Cisco adopted the Scaled Agile Framework (SAFe) and introduced three agile release trains on their Subscription Billing Platform—capabilities, defects and fixes, and projects. The idea was to collaborate on building and testing small features within one SaaS part and delivering them to the system integration and testing team.

Cisco delivered the new release of SBP on schedule and with no overtime. Defects were reduced by 40% compared to previous waterfall releases, and defect removal efficiency increased by 14%, thanks to improved team collaboration.

https://techbeacon.com/app-dev-testing/10-companies-killing-it-scaling-agile

Mark Harrison, president, and CEO at **Intermountain Healthcare** has started 15-minute huddles to keep each of the 23 hospitals in the system aligned. These huddles empower employees to communicate from the bottom-up since concerns or ideas they raise in their huddles can easily be escalated to upper management.

https://www.betterworks.com/magazine/what-is-agile-leadership-and-why-does-it-matter/

National Public Radio uses agile methods to create new programming. **John Deere** uses them to develop new machines, and **Saab** to produce new fighter jets. Intronis, a leader in cloud backup services, uses them in marketing. **Mission Bell Winery** uses them for everything from wine production to warehousing to running its senior leadership group.

As a leader you must understand and be able to use several agile methods and know which ones to use when. You must create the right conditions in the organisation for agile to work. Several companies have reallocated 25% or more of selected leaders' time from functional silos to agile leadership teams. These teams rank-order enterprise-wide portfolio backlogs, establish and coordinate agile teams elsewhere in the organization to address the highest priorities, and systematically eliminate barriers to their success. Probably the most important lesson they will all tell you is: use agile, but name one accountability point for each decision.

https://hbr.org/2016/05/embracing-agile

Is this a gap for you?

- Are you using agile methods to break work into phases?
- Are you working with cross-functional end-to-end expertise to do work?
- Are you adjusting projects and goals as the environment and strategy change?

RESOURCES

Books

THE PROFESSIONAL AGILE LEADER
THE LEADER'S JOURNEY TOWARD GROWING MATURE AGILE TEAMS AND ORGANIZATIONS

DOING
AG
ILE
RIGHT

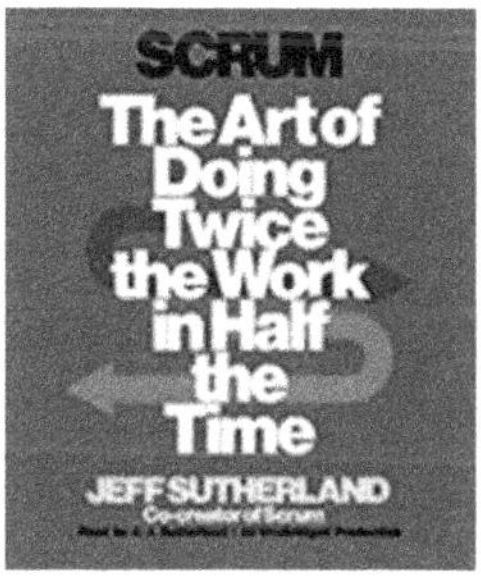
SCRUM
The Art of Doing Twice the Work in Half the Time
JEFF SUTHERLAND
Co-creator of Scrum

Videos And Podcasts

https://www.youtube.com/watch?v=WjwEh15M5Rw&t=4s What is Agile? 35 min

https://www.youtube.com/watch?v=6bifpFTyX_c 1hour25min Agile Leadership

Articles

https://hbr.org/2016/05/embracing-agile

https://www.gartner.com/en/articles/
yes-agile-sprints-can-fit-into-hybrid-work-models

FUTURE SKILL 5:

HUMAN/MACHINE OPTIMISATION AND THE SKILLS BASED APPROACH

Only 14% of business executives strongly agree that their organization is using the workforce's skills and capabilities to their fullest potential.

Cantrell et al (Deloitte whitepaper, 2022)

Sixty-one percent of business executives say new technologies such as automation and artificial intelligence (AI) that require new skills will be a primary driver of their organisation adopting a skills-based approach. Automation pushes organizations to "unfreeze" their jobs, disaggregate them into their component tasks and subtasks, and then hive off those that can be automated and reassemble the remaining tasks into a newly formed "refrozen" job. But with newer technologies continuously reshaping jobs, many are looking for new structures of organizing work that enable people to flex as needed instead of repeatedly unfreezing and freezing jobs. In this lies a real opportunity.

https://www2.deloitte.com/us/en/insights/topics/talent/organizational-skill-based-hiring.html

Humans and machines can enhance each other's strengths. To take full advantage of this collaboration, companies must understand how humans can most effectively augment machines, how machines can enhance what humans do best, and how to redesign business processes to support the partnership.

Smart machines are helping humans expand their abilities in three ways. They can amplify our cognitive strengths; interact with customers and employees to free us for higher-level tasks; and embody human skills to extend our physical capabilities. Humans must *train* machines to perform certain tasks; *explain* the outcomes of those tasks, especially when the results are counterintuitive or controversial; and *sustain* the responsible use of machines (by, for example, preventing robots from harming humans).

https://hbr.org/2018/07/collaborative-intelligence-humans-and-ai-are-joining-forces

Moxi, a robot, helps nurses with non-patient-facing tasks, such as pick up and delivering medical supplies, so nurses can focus on patient care. Moxi also decreases nurses' burnout. If AI helps with diagnosis, doctors can provide context and empathy to patients. Organisations that get this right appoint someone to study and optimise human/machine collaboration.

SEB, a major Swedish bank, now uses a virtual assistant called Aida to interact with millions of customers. Able to handle natural-language conversations, Aida has access to vast stores of data and can answer many frequently asked questions, such as how to open an account or make cross-border payments. She can also ask callers follow-up questions to solve their problems, and she's able to analyse a caller's tone of voice (frustrated versus appreciative, for example) and use that information to provide better service later. Whenever the system can't resolve an issue—which happens in about 30% of cases—it turns the caller over to a human customer-service representative and then tracks that interaction to learn how to resolve similar problems in the future. With Aida handling basic requests, human reps can concentrate on addressing more-complex issues, especially from unhappy callers who might require extra handholding.

To optimise the human-machine collaboration we must think differently about work. Ravin Jesuthasan and John Boudreau write in their book Work without Jobs: work, workers, and capabilities are shifting under leaders' feet. The era of thinking about work as a "job" and people as "job holders" is over. This is hard for leaders who grew up in a world of jobs, hierarchies, structures, function, titles, and qualifications. But the reality is the world of work is moving to a new work operating system. A system where jobs are deconstructed into tasks and projects, skills, and capabilities. This leads to more fluid and agile work reinvention, which we discussed before, and the ability to constantly recombine these components as the environment and strategy pivots require (remember those inflection points).

It also means we can stand back and ask ourselves which parts are better executed by machines (automated or augmented) than by humans (creativity, relationships, strategy).

Organisations like Unilever, Providence Health, NASA, and Cleveland Clinic have all embraced this way of working. Providence Health, facing a severe shortage of healthcare workers, built an internal talent marketplace and ecosystem by deconstructing and reconstructing all parts of jobs, qualifications, and skills. They connected this to organizations' talent and skills needs to ensure skills can be deployed differently to provide the compassionate and high-quality care they want to deliver consistently.

At **Unilever**, for example, an internal talent marketplace enables skills to fluidly move to projects and tasks across the organization, either as a permanent employee or as a "U-Worker": a worker who has a guaranteed minimum retainer along with a core set of benefits, and who contracts with Unilever for short-term projects. Explains Patrick Hull, vice president of future of work at Unilever, "We just see that there's all this opportunity that we can unlock for people that maybe we wouldn't have been considering because, as with many organizations, we would have been more in our functional silos." Departmental work at Unilever is increasingly divided into projects, tasks, and deliverables.

https://www2.deloitte.com/us/en/insights/topics/talent/organizational-skill-based-hiring.html

Cleveland Clinic, for example, moved from being organized by medical specialties and specific job titles such as "doctor" or "nurse" to broadly defining all staff as "caregivers" responsible for treating not just physical illnesses but also patients' spirit and emotions. Instead of organising departments based on the medical specializations, groups were formed around the patients and their illnesses, creating multidisciplinary, collaborative teams—which also sparked innovation in new treatments.

https://www2.deloitte.com/us/en/insights/topics/talent/organizational-skill-based-hiring.html

Is this a gap for you?

- Have you deconstructed and reconstructed jobs to understand what would be better done by machines and what would be better done by humans?
- Have you built an organisation wide skills ontology and mapped your people to it?
- Have you built an ongoing upskilling and reskilling approach to address skills gaps?
- Are you deploying skills to the right opportunities through agile work and internal talent marketplaces?

RESOURCES

Books

Ravin Jesuthasan and John W. Boudreau
WORK
WITHOUT
JOBS
How to Reboot Your Organization's Work Operating System

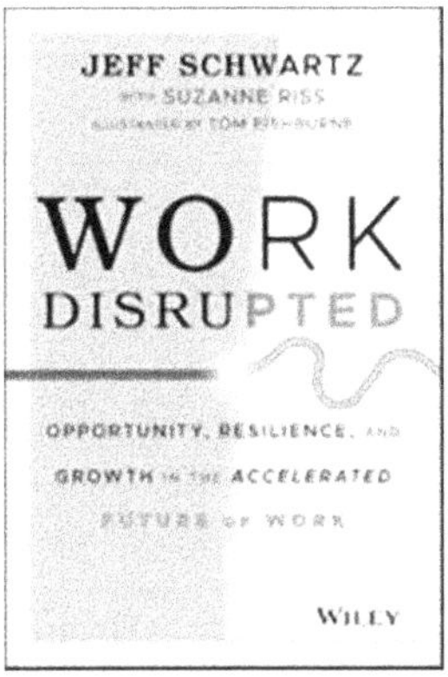
JEFF SCHWARTZ
WORK
DISRUPTED
WILEY

Articles

https://hbr.org/2018/07/collaborative-intelligence-humans-and-ai-are-joining-forces

https://www2.deloitte.com/us/en/insights/topics/talent/organizational-skill-based-hiring.html

https://www.mckinsey.com/capabilities/people-and-organizational-performance/our-insights/taking-a-skills-based-approach-to-building-the-future-workforce

FUTURE SKILL 6:

STORYTELLING

Stories are the single most powerful weapon in a leader's arsenal.

Howard Gardner

To change the culture, change the nature of the conversations across the company.

And put stories to be at the heart of those conversations.

Imagine if your entire organisation is discussing the same story at the same time, say every month. Imagine the gradual but robust understanding everyone would have about what the values mean. And by telling their own stories (because hearing a story invariably prompts other stories to be told) they will, over time, begin to really own these values. They are no longer a set of abstract ideas handed down by the head office.

Shawn Callahan

Leaders shape culture. To change the culture, change the nature of the conversations across the organisation. And put stories at the heart of those conversations. When you tell stories, your words and decisions turn into colour. Telling a compelling story is how you build credibility for yourself and your ideas. Use stories to create clarity and alignment.

It is a learned skill that can shift employees' mindsets by suspending beliefs and introducing new ideas, and it lets leaders communicate their vision to guide employees in the right direction.

Telling stories—sequences of events that appeal to our senses and have a surprise—is a natural way to pass information to the brain. All this information is stored as sequences: as you move through the world, your brain perceives what's happening and continually predicts what will happen next. Telling a well-structured story means encoding a new sequence into a listener's brain without them having experienced these events. This is how we learn, are inspired, and begin to imagine new things.

We might think of culture as the neural patterns of the organisation. Stories illustrating and reinforcing vision and strategy are an important conduit in creating new neural pathways at a company level (c.f. new organisational mindsets). Stories inspire people to change. They write: "Because sharing important information by using a story is more memorable, and the first story often wins, it is imperative that leaders take the time to craft and test their stories. That way, the right information will be given at the right time, and it will land in the manner intended." (Grundel et al, 2022)

Shawn Callahan, the author of *Putting Stories to Work*, is a thought leader I follow in building storytelling capability and consulting. He proposes using systematic and structured storytelling to clarify strategy, embed company values and drive change. He believes the clarity stories and tackling anti-stories are key to energising people. Success stories keep people going.

Clarity stories can tell strategy as a story. While creating the clarity story, leaders also need to address the stories that can derail the strategy or transformation – anti-stories. One anti-story we hear often is" "We have done this before, and it did not work". Replace them with powerful clarity stories. A clarity story has four components: past context and results; a change and its impacts; new responsive behaviours needed; and future actions and success factors. It helps a leader get a new strategy to stick. You can also use influence stories. When an "anti-story" is discovered, acknowledge and tackle it. The influence narrative then shares a story with the opposite viewpoint, supports the new perspective, and calls action. An influence story doesn't push data at the listener; it lets the listener pull the new meaning into their worldview by seeding doubts about the old worldview and becoming open to alternate realities.

Case in point where storytelling was adopted to help with communication of values powerfully is Volvo. **Volvo**, a leading transport giant, curated stories by 107 employees from across its global locations on its core values driving organizational culture. These stories are stories of the employees' own experiences of working at Volvo and represent Volvo's people and values as an organization. 35 of these stories are released through DVDs and books. The 'Volvo way' stories is to inspire people and support the organization's goals. These stories were a powerful communication tool that helped in creating a common culture and shared values across its offices worldwide, which is important for a global company like Volvo. (Ghandi, K., 2017).

Is this a gap for you?

- Do you use storytelling as a leader?
- Have you been trained in storytelling techniques?

RESOURCES

Books

PUTTING
STORIES
TO
WORK
SHAWN CALLAHAN

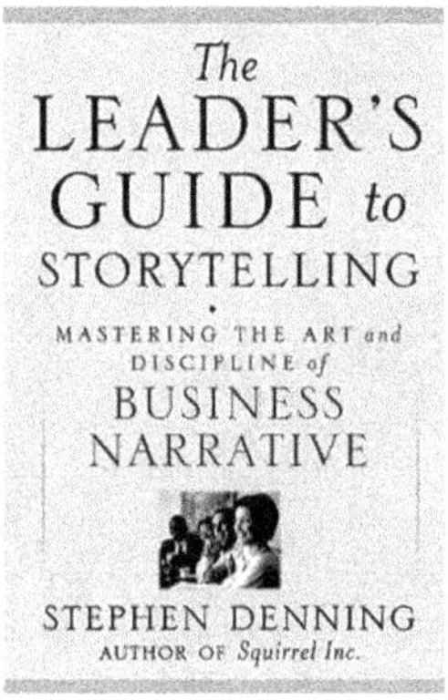
The
LEADER'S
GUIDE to
STORYTELLING
MASTERING THE ART and
DISCIPLINE of
BUSINESS
NARRATIVE
STEPHEN DENNING
AUTHOR OF Squirrel Inc.

Articles

https://hbr.org/2020/10/

storytelling-can-make-or-break-your-leadership

Videos And Podcasts

https://www.youtube.com/watch?v=QaIeIRf1H8k Shawn Callaghan 4:10

CHAPTER 12

The Ongoing Work Of The Leader: Learning, Connecting, Achieving

You are doing your sprints, and you are learning, relating and achieving every day. This must become part of the way you do things now. Leadership is not an additional task – it is how you show up daily, what you focus on and how you spend your time.

Writing this book and interviewing these incredible leaders and organisations gave me renewed hope that a different way of leading in the future of work is possible. I recently read the book *Ruthlessly Caring*, which resonated with everything my research and interviewees told me. Author Amy Cohen (2023) explains the paradoxical nature of the leadership required. It requires the unfreezing of your leadership identity as described before. You need to become able to flex, evolve and expand to lead in increasing complexity. Amy spells out the five most common paradoxical mindsets. They are presented on the next page.

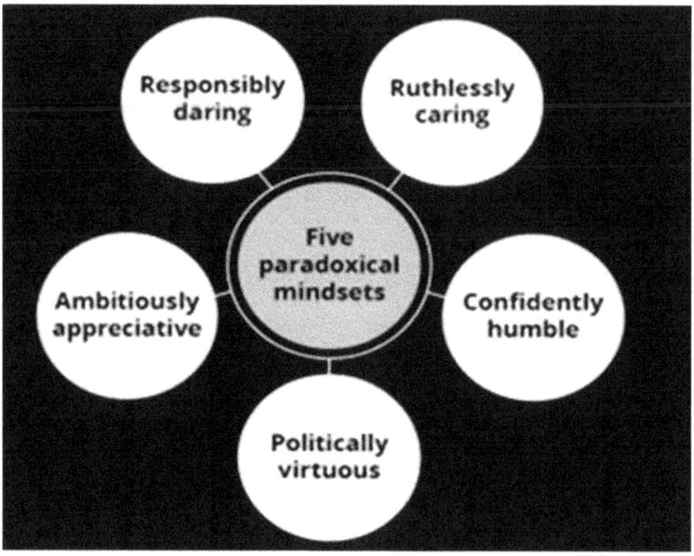
Responsibly daring
Ruthlessly caring
Five paradoxical mindsets
Ambitiously appreciative
Confidently humble
Politically virtuous

Cohen, 2023

1. Ruthlessly caring is about being performance and results-driven and making tough decisions whilst showing deep care for people and treating them with compassion and respect.

2. Ambitiously appreciative is about being driven and achieving but always retaining a sense of perspective and an appreciation of life outside of work.

3. Politically virtuous leaders are savvy, can influence and network, but are grounded in their values and integrity and are transparent and honest with people.

4. Confidently humble leaders are decisive, self-assured, and open about their limitations and learning. They genuinely value others' ideas and opinions.

5. Responsibly daring leaders are bold, set tough goals, and strive to improve the business for the future. They are also realistic and take responsible risks.

The leaders I interviewed all showed the ability to work with these paradoxes. They have great humility and show up in very human and approachable ways. They are driven by making a difference, not by the title or status. They all moved on from their roles at the right time, not clinging to power.

They are infinitely curious, open and adaptable. They make time for reading, listening to podcasts and speaking to others with different views and perspectives. They are comfortable with not having all the answers or being seen as the hero or expert and willing to just try something, experiment, learn something new or take just one step. They are also open about their mistakes and what they learnt from them.

They are comfortable with the idea of AND – that two things can be true at once and they do not have to choose between things like performance and wellbeing, for example. They do not expect things to be simple and linear. All are also fearful of new things and change, but they are all more fearful of things not changing, so they step forward with courage and sometimes stand in very lonely places as the sole voice for a cause. They will back themselves and others and they have a 'can do' attitude. They are also willing to make tough and sometimes uncomfortable decisions when needed.

They spend a lot of time with their people and listening to their people. They let ideas flow from everywhere in their organisations, especially from those closest to the customer. They build relationships all the time and value how diversity creates better performance. They spend time with and leverage their organization's talent and focus intentionally on collaboration.

They manage their energy, focus and wellness. They all have daily exercise routines, mental space, healthy eating and good sleep. They show up as calm helping to put others at ease. Most importantly, they do not tolerate moral and value behaviours misaligned or threaten psychological safety and team effectiveness.

Deborah Ancona (2006) sums it up well. Leadership is not an individual sport. Leadership is a process of creating change and it develops over time. You need to continue to make sense of the internal and external environments you operate in, intentionally develop the key relationships within and across the organisation, build and communicate a clear direction and create new ways of doing things.

The organisations shifting their leadership development approaches have made a clear shift away from the competency, trait-based and one-off leadership events way of developing people and instead are focusing on mindsets and practices leaders can develop collectively over time and in context. They are providing multiple ways for people to engage in ongoing learning and use real organisational challenges as part of the learning processes. Work is learning and learning is work. Most importantly, they understand human development, habit change and brain development and utilise pedagogical and transformative learning methods fit for purpose.

Bonus Items

To enhance your user experience of this book, I created these complimentary bonus resources for you.

To access them, please email marianne@rouxconsulting.org.

Bonus item 1: Download and print a complimentary copy of a workbook covering the areas addressed with lots of space for recording your insights, key takeaways and action items.

Bonus item 2: A complimentary ebook of the Behaviours and Practices to reinforce your learning.

Bibliography

Chapter 1

Sources

- Daft, R.L. (2008). *The Leadership Experience.* Thomson Southwestern.
- Hooper, D., (2003). *Paradox and Ambiguity vs Clarity.* Accessed at https://www.buildingfutureleaders.com/uploads/4/1/1/4/411493/paradox_and_ambiguity_vs_clarity.pdf
- Pfeffer, J. (2016). *Getting beyond the BS of leadership literature.* McKinsey Quarterly, January 2016.
- Pontefract, D.(2023). *New Research Suggests An Alarming Decline in High-Quality Leaders.* Accessed at https://www.forbes.com/sites/danpontefract/2023/02/08/new-research-suggests-an-alarming-decline-in-high-quality-leaders/?sh=58fc21f51493.

Chapter 2

Sources

- Ackerman, P. L., & Kanfer, R. (2020). Work in the 21st century: New directions for aging and adult development.

American Psychologist, 75(4), 486 498. https://doi.org/10.1037/amp0000615

- Boyden Executive Survey, (2022), *Strengthening the human centric core of Industry 5.0.* Accessed at (https://www.boyden.com/media/strengthening-the-human-centric-core-of-industry-50-27765859/index.html)
- Cambon, A. & Walker, G. (2021). *Gartner Future of work report ebook*, August 2021. Accessed at gartner.com/en/insights/future-of-work.
- Jesuthasan, R.& Boudreau , J. (2022). *Work without jobs.* The MIT Press.
- Kerr, W.R., Billaud, E. & Hjortshoej, M.F. (2020) *Unilever's Response to the Future of Work.* Harvard Business School, 28 Oct 2020.
- Kraaijenbrink, J. (2022). *What is industry 5.0 and how it will radically change your business strategy*. Accessed at https://www.forbes.com/sites/jeroenkraaijenbrink/2022/05/24/what-is-industry-50-and-how-it-will-radically-change-your-business-strategy/?sh=7129dd3b20bd)
- Qualtrics (2023). *Redefining the future of work.* Accessed at https://www.qualtrics.com/blog/redefining-the-future-of-work/.
- Robleck, V., Meskp, M. & Krapez, A. (2016). *A Complex View of Industry 4.0.* SAGE Open, April-June 2016, 1-11.
- Schwartz, J. & Riss, S. (2021). *Work Disrupted.* Wiley.

- Skytland, N. (2018) *The Future of Work Framework at NASA.* Accessed at https://blogs.nasa.gov/futureofwork/author/nskytlan/.
- Strauss,D.(2023).GenerativeAisettoaffect300mjobsacrossmajor economies. Accessed at https://www.ft.com/ content/7dec4483-ad34-4007-bb3a-7ac925643999?shareType=nongift.Sources

Chapter 3

Sources

- Cook-Greuter, S. R., (2004). Making the Case for a Developmental Perspective, *Industrial and Commercial Training*, 36 (7).
- Dawson, T.K. (2015). *LAP certification, 2015*. Lectica.live.
- Dall'Alba, G. (2009). Learning to be professionals. New York, NY: Springer.
- DeRue, D.S. & Myers, C.G. (2014). Leadership development: A review and agenda for future research. In: *Oxford Handbook of Leadership and Organizations*. Chapter 37. Oxford: Oxford University Press, 832-855.
- Kegan, R. (1982). The evolving self. Cambridge, MA: Harvard University Press.
- Mabey, C. (2013). Leadership development in organisations: Multiple discourses and diverse practices. *International Journal of Management Review*, 15, 359-380.

- Petrie, N. (2014). *Future trends in leadership development.* Center for Creative Leadership. Retrieved from http://www.ccl.org/wp-content/uploads/2015/04/futureTrends.pdf.
- Rabinowitz, N. (2023). *1% better.* Accessed at https://www.linkedin.com/pulse/1-better-noah-g-rabinowitz/.
- Russon, C.& Reinelt, C.(2004).The results of an evaluation scan of 55 leadership development programs. *Journal of Leadership and Organizational Studies*, 10 (3), 104-107.
- Van Seters, D. A. & Field, R. H. G. (1990). The evolution of leadership theory.*Journal of Organisational Change Management.* December 1990, 29-45.
- Veldsman, T. (2017). *Re inventing Leadership Development for a different, future world.* STOP-OVER 27. Accessed at https://www.linkedin.com/pulse/leadership-universe-27-re-inventing-development-theo-veldsman/.
- Vince, R. & Pedler, M. (2018). Putting the contradictions back into leadership development. *Leadership and Organization Development Journal*, 39 (7), 859-872.
- Vogel, B., Reichard, R.J., Batistic, S. & Cerne, M. (2020). A bibliometric review of the leadership development field: How we got here, where we are, and where we are headed. *The Leadership Quarterly*, https:/doi.org/10.1016/leaqua2020.101381.
- Zhu, J., Song, L.J., Zhu, L. & Johnson, R.E. (2019). Visualizing the landscape and evolution of leadership research. *The Leadership Quarterly*, 30, 215-232.

Chapter 4

Sources

- Bailey, S. (2021) The future of work is forcing an evolution in leadership. Accessed at https://www.fastcompany.com/90708347/the-future-of-work-is-forcing-an-evolution-in-leadership
- Billies, T. (2015). How to be a great leader in a complex world. Accessed at https://www.weforum.org/agenda/2015/01/ great-leader-in-complex-world/.
- Cook-Greuter, S. R., (2004). Making the Case for a Developmental Perspective, *Industrial and Commercial Training*, 36 (7).
- Day, D. V., Harrison, M. M., and Halpin, S. M. (2009). *An Integrative Approach to Leader Development: Connecting Adult Development, Identity, and Expertise.* New York, NY: Psychology Press.
- Gloor, P.A. (2017). Swarm Leadership and the Collective Mind. Emerald Publishing.
- Kelly, R.(2019). Constructing Leadership 4.0. Swarm leadership and the Fourth Industrial Revolution. Kindle edition.
- Yammarino, F. J., Salas, E., Serban, A., Shirreffs, K., & Shuffler, M. L. (2012). Collectivistic leadership approaches: Putting the "we" in leadership science and practice. *Industrial and Organizational Psychology*, 5, 382–402.

Chapter 5

Sources

- Cook-Greuter, S. R., (2004). Making the Case for a Developmental Perspective, Industrial and Commercial Training, Volume 36, Number 7.
- Kegan, R. and Lahey, L. (2009). Immunity to Change. Harvard Business Review Press.
- Lang, A. (2018). Six Keys to designing a learning journey for leaders. A DDI article. Retrieved from http://www.ddiworld.com/DDI/media/articles/sixkeystodesigningalearningjourneyforleaders_ar_ddi.pdf?ext=.pdf.

Chapter 6

Sources

- Ancona, D. (2012) Sensemaking: Framing and action in the unknown. Published in The handbook for teaching leadership : knowing, doing, and being. - Los Angeles [u.a.]: SAGE Publications, ISBN 1-4129-9094-7. - 2012, p. 3-19.
- Kutz M.R. (2010). Leadership in athletic training: implication for practice and education in allied health care, *Journal of Allied Health*, ISSN 0090-7421, 39(4), 265-279.
- Kutz, M, (2013) Contextual Intelligence. Lulu.com.
- Kutz M.R. (2008b). Toward a conceptual model of contextual intelligence: A transferable leadership construct. *Leadership Review*, 8, 18-31, http://www.leadershipreview.org/2008winter/article2.pdf.

- Lagerstedt, E. (2020). At an inflection point? Accessed at https:// elisabetlagerstedt.com/2020/08/07/at-an-inflection-point/.
- McGrath, R. (2019). *Seeing around corners*. Mariner Books.

Chapter 7

Sources

- Bourton, S, Lavoie, J., & Vogel, T. (2018) Leading with inner agility, McKinsey Quarterly, accessed at https://www.mckinsey.com/capabilities/people-and-organizational-performance/our-insights/leading-with-inner-agility.
- Carden, J, Jones, R.J. & Passmore, J. (2021). Defining Self Awareness in the Context of Adult Development: A Systematic Literature Review. Journal of Management Education. Accessed at https://journals.sagepub.com/doi/full/10.1177/1052562921990065.
- Cohen, A. W. (2023). Ruthlessly Caring and other Paradoxical Mindsets. Wiley.
- David, S. (2017). Emotional Agility, Penguin.
- David, D. & Congleton, C. (2013). Emotional Agility. Harvard Business Review, November 2013.
- Duckworth, A. (2017). Grit: Why passion and resilience are the secrets to success. Vermillion.
- Dweck, C. S. (2008). *Mindset*. New York, NY: Random House Digital Inc.

- Eurich, T. (2018). What Self Awareness really is (and how to cultivate it). Harvard Business Review, January 2018.
- Flaum, J.P. (2018). When it comes to Business Leadership, Nice Guys finish first. Accessed at https://greenpeakpartners.com/wp-content/uploads/2018/09/Green-Peak_Cornell-University-Study_What-predicts-success.pdf.
- George, B. & Sims, (2007). True North: Discover Your Authentic Leadership. John Wiley & Sons.
- Newport, C. (2016). Deep Work. Piatkus.
- Warner, C.T. (2019). What We Are. Accessed at https://arbingerinstitute.de/Download/Whitepaper_What_We_Are.pdf.
- Zoldan, A. (2018). 5 Ways to Build Grit and Perseverance Across Your Team, Accessed at https://www.inc.com/ari-zoldan/why-gut-instinct-still-matters-for-entrepreneurs-in-a-data-driven-world.html.

Chapter 8

Sources

- Cohen, A. W. (2023). Ruthlessly Caring and other Paradoxical Mindsets. Wiley.
- Copeland, Mary Kay (2014). The Emerging Significance of Values Based Leadership: A Literature Review. *International Journal of Leadership Studies* 8.2, 105-135.
- Daft, R.L. (2008). *The Leadership Experience*. Thomson South Western.

- Kedzierski, B. (2022). The Rise of ESG and What it Means for Your Leadership.
- https://www.industrialtransformationnetwork.com/ energy-management-sustainability/articles/the-rise-of-esg-and-what-it-means-for-your-leadership.
- Mathieson, K. (2003). Elements of Moral Maturity. Journal of College and Character. 4 (5), DOI:10.2202/1940-1639.1356
- McLeod, S. (2013) Kohlberg's Theory of Moral Development, Accessed at https://www.simplypsychology.org/kohlberg.html.
- Sekerka, L. E., & Bagozzi, R. P. (2007). Moral courage in the workplace: Moving to and from the desire and decision to act. *Business Ethics: A European Review, 16*(2), 132–149. https://doi.org/10.1111/j.1467-8608.2007.00484.x.

Chapter 9

Sources

- Billies, T. (2015). How to be a great leader in a complex world. Accessed at https://www.weforum.org/agenda/2015/01/ great-leader-in-complex-world/.
- Cohen, A. W. (2023). Ruthlessly Caring and other Paradoxical Mindsets. Wiley.
- Cooke-Greuter, S. Accessed at https://www.sloww.co/ ego-development-theory-cook-greuter/.
- Day, D. V., Gronn, P., & Salas, E. (2004). Leadership capacity in teams. The Leadership Quarterly, 15(6), 857–880. https://doi.org/10.1016/j.leaqua.2004.09.001.

- Garvey-Berger, J.G. & Achi, G. (2020). Understanding the leader's 'identity mindtrap': Personal growth for the C-suite. McKinsey Quarterly. Accessed at https://www.mckinsey.com/capabilities/people-and-organizational-performance/our-insights/understanding-the-leaders-identity-mindtrap-personal-growth-for-the-c-suite.
- Heifetz, R., Grashow, A. & Linksky, M. (2009). The Practice of Adaptive Leadership. Harvard Business Review Press.
- Rooke, & Torbert (2005). Seven Transformations of Leadership. Harvard Business Review, Accessed at https://hbr.org/2005/04/seven-transformations-of-leadership.

Chapter 10

Sources

- Billies, T. (2015). How to be a great leader in a complex world. Accessed at https://www.weforum.org/agenda/2015/01/ great-leader-in-complex-world/.
- Cross, R. Davenport, T.H. & Cantrell, S. (2003). The Social Side of Performance. *MIT Sloan Management Review,* Fall 2003.
- Edmondson, A.C., Jang, S, & Casciaro, T. (2019). *Cross-Silo Leadership*. Harvard Business Review, May-June 2019.
- Ibarra, H. & Hunter, M.L. (2007). How Leaders Create and Use Network. Harvard Business Review. January 2007.
- Ibarra, H. & Hansen, M.T. (2015). Are you a collaborative leader? Harvard Business Review. Accessed at https://www.researchgate.net/publication/51531846_Are_you_a_collaborative_leader

- Oxford Leadership, 2017. Collaborative Leadership. White Paper. Accessed at https://www.oxfordleadership.com/wp-content/uploads/2017/07/OL-White-Paper-Collaborative-Leadership.pdf
- White, M. & Winkworth, G. (2012). A Rubric for Building Effective Collaboration: Creating and Sustaining Multi Service Level Partnerships To Improve Outcomes for Clients. ISBN. 0987356410, 9780987356413.

Chapter 11

Sources

- Avolio, B.J., Sosik, J.J., Kahai, S.S. & Baker, B. (2014). E-leadership: Re-examining transformations in leadership source and transmission. The Leadership Quarterly, 25 (1), 105-131.
- Autor, Mindell, and Reynolds "Work of the Future".
- Benton, A. (2023). Quotes on Agile/Scrum. Accessed at https://andreab.me/library/agile-scrum-kanban/agile-scrum-kanban-quotes/.
- Beverly, D. (2016). The Best Article You have ever read about Brain Based Coaching. Accessed at https://www.linkedin.com/pulse/best-article-youve-ever-read-brain-based-coaching-dan-beverly/.
- Business Chief (2022). Future of work – why a human-centred approach is key.

Accessed at https://businesschief.eu/leadership-and-strategy/future-of-work-why-a-human-centred-approach-is-key.

- Chavez, M. & Paulse, S. (2020). Rehumanising leadership. LID Publishing.
- Fergusson, L. (2019). The nature of work-related problems: messy, co-produced and wicked. Journal of Work-Applied Management, 11 (2), 106-120.
- Ghandi, K., (2017). Storytelling to build values.
- Grint, K. (2008). Wicked Problems and Clumsy Solutions: The role of leadership. Clinical Leader, Volume I Number II, December 2008, ISSN 1757-3424, BAMM Publications.
- Grundel, R., Callaghan, S., Schenk, M. & Adams, M, (2022). The Science of Storytelling. Accessed at https://www.anecdote.com/2022/03/science-of-storytelling/.
- Johansen, B. (2017) The New Leadership Literacies: Thriving in a Future of Extreme Disruption and Distributed Everything. Berret-Koehler.
- Kang, J. (2020). Do we do enough problem finding before problem solving? Accessed at https://uxdesign.cc/ problem-finding-before-problem-solving-4aaaa8bdb889.
- Rock, D. (2006). A Brain-Based Approach to Coaching. International Journal of Coaching in Organizations, 2006, 4(2), 32-43.
- Shinn, S. (2022). Developing Tech-Savvy Leaders.

Access at https://www.aacsb.edu/insights/articles/2022/05/developing-tech-savvy-leaders

Chapter 12

Sources

Ancona, D. (2006). Leadership in the Age of Uncertainty. The Systems Thinker, 17 (7), September 2006.

Cohen, A. W. (2023). Ruthlessly Caring and other Paradoxical Mindsets. Wiley.

Appendix 1

Chapter 6

Tools

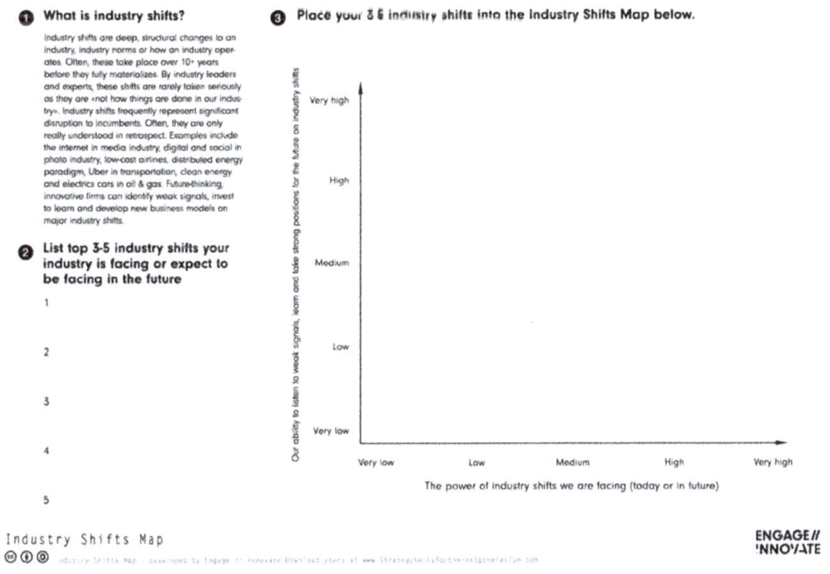

What is industry shifts?
Industry shifts are deep, structural changes to an industry, industry norms or how an industry operates. Often, these take place over 10+ years before they fully materializes. By industry leaders and experts, these shifts are rarely taken seriously as they are «not how things are done in our industry». Industry shifts frequently represent significant disruption to incumbents. Often, they are only really understood in retrospect. Examples include the internet in media industry, digital and social in photo industry, low-cost airlines, distributed energy paradigm, Uber in transportation, clean energy and electrics cars in oil & gas. Future-thinking, innovative firms can identify weak signals, invest to learn and develop new business models on major industry shifts.
List top 3-5 industry shifts your industry is facing or expect to be facing in the future
1
2
3
4
5
Place your 3-5 industry shifts into the Industry Shifts Map below.
Our ability to listen to weak signals, learn and take strong positions for the future on industry shifts
Very high
High
Medium
Low
Very low
Very low
Low
Medium
High
Very high
The power of industry shifts we are facing (today or in future)
Industry Shifts Map
ENGAGE//
INNOVATE

Map your industry shifts

https://www.strategytools.io/strategy-tools/industry-shifts-map/

Chapter 7

Growth Mindset

Tools

Switch your thoughts and language

FROM	TO
This is too hard	This challenge is a learning opportunity
I cannot do this	I cannot do this yet
This does not work	This does not work yet
I can't make mistakes	Mistakes help me learn

Self-Awareness

Tools

Complete a 360 assessment

https://leadershipcircle.com/leadership-assessment-tools/ leadership-circle-profile/

Know your strengths

The Free Via Character Strengths Survey

https://www.viacharacter.org

Define your best possible self-using this worksheet.

https://www2.winona.edu/resilience/Media/Best-Possible-Self-Worksheet.pdf

Grit

Tools

Expert – or deliberate – practice is one concrete tool that gritty people use to master a skill or improve their performance.

Steps of Expert Practice
CharacterLAB
Decide on a small sub-skill to practice
Practice with 100% focus
Get feedback and reflect
Repeat!

Source: CharacterLab Expert Practice Playbook

Emotional Agility

Tools

Practice unhooking from unhelpful emotions, thoughts, and reactions

Developing emotional agility helps us overcome the hooks that commonly intrude on our thoughts, emotions, and stories to dominate our behaviour in ways contrary to our well-being. Rather than ignoring them and pretending we're always happy and that everything is fine, emotional agility gives us the resilience to identify and accept the feelings that stress us out and put strategies to use them to our advantage.

To embrace change positively and experience positive emotions surrounding these changes, we must be emotionally agile, shifting our mindset to the new situation at hand. (Susan David). We need to reframe and unhook. Reframing is seeing the current situation from a different perspective, which can be tremendously helpful in problem solving, decision making and learning.

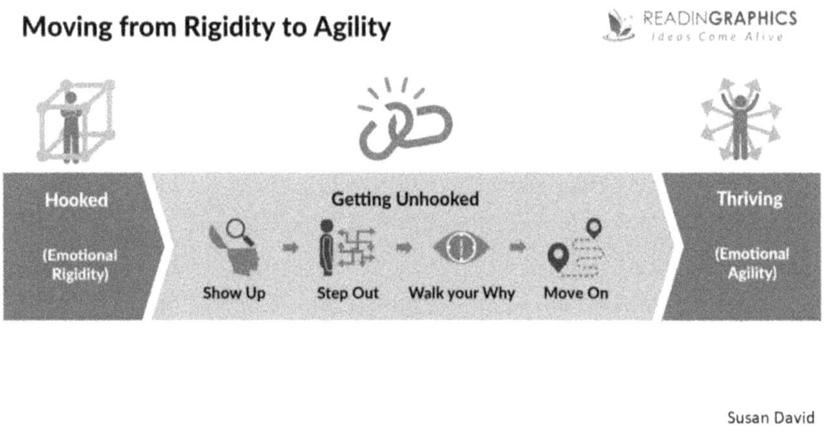
Moving from Rigidity to Agility
READINGGRAPHICS
Ideas Come Alive
Hooked
(Emotional Rigidity)
Getting Unhooked
Show Up
Step Out
Walk your Why
Move On
Thriving
(Emotional Agility)
Susan David

David, 2017

Focus and Deep Work

Tools And Practices

Set Only Three Main Objectives For The Day

A long list of things to do can feel insurmountable and overwhelm us. We're ready to give up before we start, and that's when it becomes easy to give in to distractions. You can offset this by giving yourself three objectives to accomplish every day. Write them on a sticky note and post it where you can see it every time you look up from your work.

Timeboxing

Timeboxing is a simple technique to manage time and become more productive. The idea is to give a certain amount of time to an activity in advance and then complete the activity within that time frame. There are two types of time boxes: "hard time boxes" and "soft time boxes". The terms hard and soft refer to how you handle the end of a time box:

When a soft time box ends, you allow the current point in discussion or the current task at work to finish. When a hard time box ends, you drop everything, stop doing what you do, take a break, or move on to the next point on the agenda.

Anchor Task

Choose an anchor task. One of the major improvements I've made recently is to assign one (and only one) priority to each workday. The power of choosing one priority is that it naturally guides your behaviour by forcing you to organize your life around that responsibility.

Power Hour

Eliminate the distractions of email, instant messaging, phones, radio, and anything else that will take your attention. Then work on one project for 60 minutes.

Fixed Schedule Productivity

Embrace "fixed-schedule productivity". Rather than working ridiculous hours to accomplish your goals, constrain yourself to a typical eight-hour workday that forces you to be ruthless choosing where to spend your time and energy.

Change Your Approach To Email

Reduce the back-and-forth of emails with a "process-centric approach to email". By sending more thorough and complete correspondence, you'll close the loop on a conversation more quickly. And not every email that lands in your inbox requires a response.

Chapter 8

Tools

The US Army Ethical Triangle

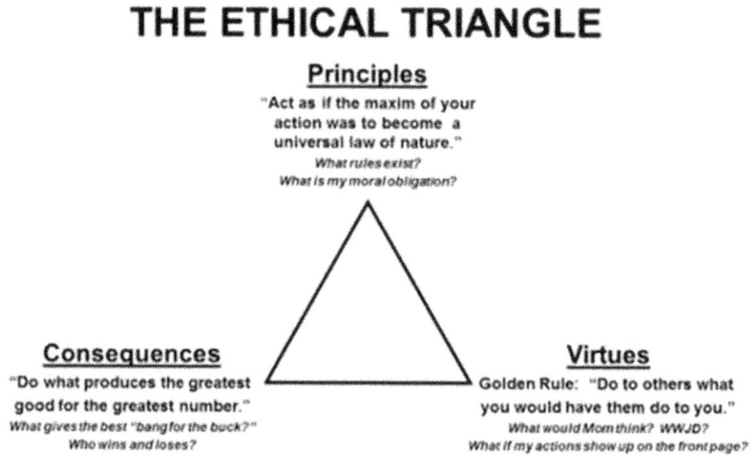
THE ETHICAL TRIANGLE
Principles
"Act as if the maxim of your action was to become a universal law of nature."
What rules exist?
What is my moral obligation?
Consequences
"Do what produces the greatest good for the greatest number."
What gives the best "bang for the buck?"
Who wins and loses?
Virtues
Golden Rule: "Do to others what you would have them do to you."
What would Mom think? WWJD?
What if my actions show up on the front page?

https://www.civilaffairsassoc.org/post/copy-of-army-special-forces-and-ethics

Steps when facing a dilemma

Here is an ethical decision-making process you can use. Identify a moral or ethical dilemma you are dealing with right now and work through the steps.

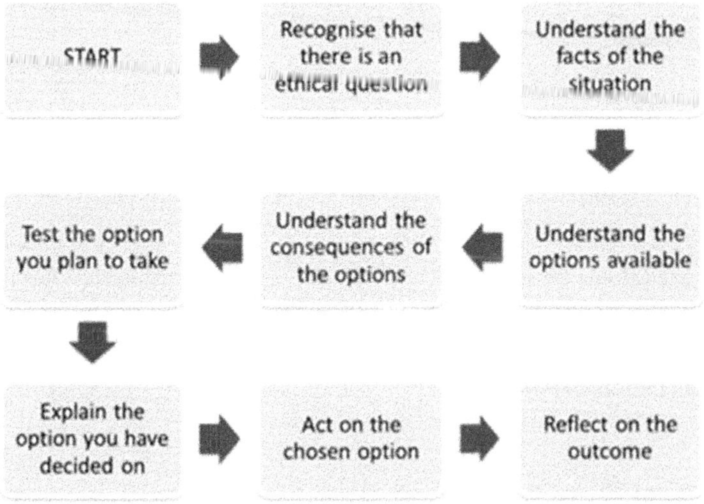
START
Recognise that there is an ethical question
Understand the facts of the situation
Understand the options available
Understand the consequences of the options
Test the option you plan to take
Explain the option you have decided on
Act on the chosen option
Reflect on the outcome

https://www.iaa.govt.nz/for-advisers/adviser-tools/ethics-toolkit/solving- ethical-problems/

Chapter 9

Tools And Practices

Grow your mind

Here are three questions to help you grow:

1. Why do I believe what I believe? Stop looking for evidence to support your beliefs, and instead try looking for their sources. Did a belief come from an external authority in a socialized way? Did you

write it yourself, basing it on your principles or values? As you examine your belief system, you can shift your attachment to your current form of mind.

2. How could I be wrong? This question isn't meant to help you make your beliefs bulletproof but to open them up so you recognize other ways of seeing the world that might help you—and might be as true as your own vision. The discomfort you feel at this process ("I can't be wrong!") means you're on the right track. Keep going; this practice creates psychological flexibility and opens us up to new possibilities.

3. Who do I want to be next? Will I be less reactive? Will I have a bigger view If we have a sense of this new person we are growing into, it will be easier to spot—and avoid—the identity mind trap and continue to walk through our development path with grace.

Garvey Berger & Achi, in McKinsey Quarterly, 2020

Chapter 10

Tools

<u>Cross silo dialogues</u>

Instead of one-way and silo, function-based information sessions, set up cross-silo discussions and look at the world together through the eyes of the customer. Do this in person. An example is "focused event analysis" (FEA) at Children's Minnesota. In an FEA, people from the health system's different clinical and operational groups come together after a failure, such as the administration of the wrong medication to a patient. One at a time, participants offer their take on what happened; the goal is to carefully document multiple perspectives *before* trying to identify a cause. Often participants are surprised to learn how people from other groups saw the incident. The assumption underlying the FEA is that most failures have not one root cause but many. Once the folks involved have a multifunctional picture of the contributing factors, they can change procedures and systems to prevent similar failures. (Edmondson et al, 2019)

The collaboration rubric

Be strategic and deliberate in identifying the collaborators brought in to help solve a problem and the level of collaboration required from them.

Use the collaboration rubric to plan your collaboration (White & Winkworth, 2012).

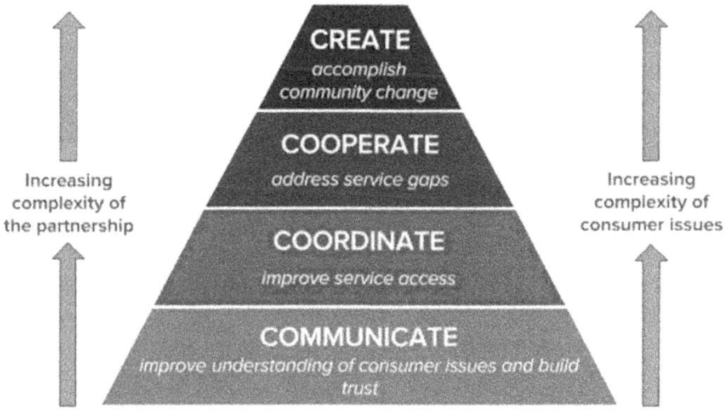
CREATE
accomplish community change
COOPERATE
address service gaps
COORDINATE
improve service access
COMMUNICATE
improve understanding of consumer issues and build trust
Increasing complexity of the partnership
Increasing complexity of consumer issues

https://www.successfulcollaborations.com.au/the-collaboration-rubric

Chapter 11

Complex Problem Finding and Solving (Critical Thinking)

Tools

What are the wicked problems to resolve and paradoxes you should reconcile with Both/And thinking?

How can you resolve them? A helpful tool is Polarity Mapping (As proposed by CCL). You can use Polarity Mapping to:

- Articulate 2 "poles" that are competing or at odds.
- Look at the potential positive results (and the negatives).
- Explore the drawbacks or fears related to over-emphasizing one or the other.

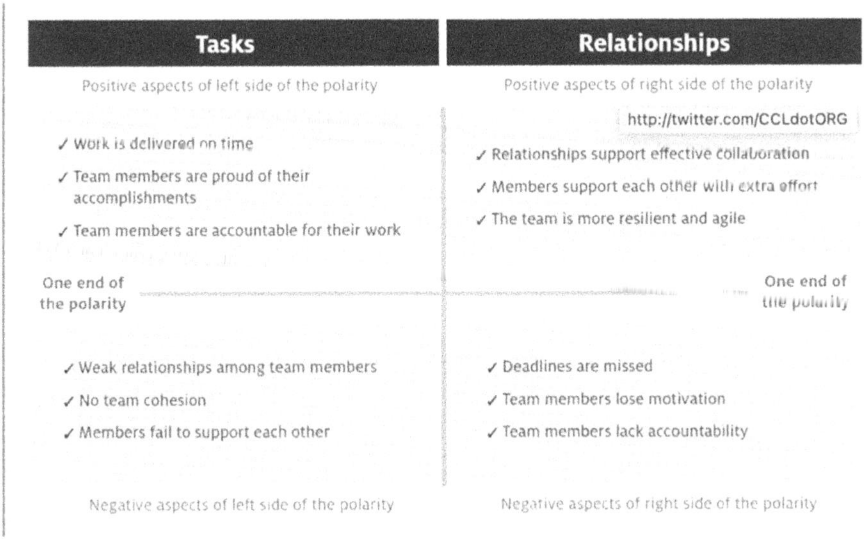
Tasks
Relationships
Positive aspects of left side of the polarity
Positive aspects of right side of the polarity
http://twitter.com/CCLdotORG
✓ Work is delivered on time
✓ Team members are proud of their accomplishments
✓ Team members are accountable for their work
✓ Relationships support effective collaboration
✓ Members support each other with extra effort
✓ The team is more resilient and agile
One end of the polarity
One end of the polarity
✓ Weak relationships among team members
✓ No team cohesion
✓ Members fail to support each other
✓ Deadlines are missed
✓ Team members lose motivation
✓ Team members lack accountability
Negative aspects of left side of the polarity
Negative aspects of right side of the polarity

https://www.ccl.org/articles/leading-effectively-articles/ manage-paradox-for-better-performance/

I use a complex problem dissolving method I learnt from Biomatrix theory (http://www.biomatrixtheory.com). I map the mess with a group of diverse stakeholders, we identify the patterns in the mess, and we then brainstorm solutions (ideate the ideal future) before we back cast to the where we are now to figure out how to tackle the complex problem.

Mess Mapping is a powerful process and analytic tool for helping stakeholders resolve Wicked Problems. Mess mapping uses visual mapping to map all we know about the problem so we can arrive to a shared understanding of it. Mess Map diagram or mural represents a common mental model of the problem at hand that shows the important "chunks" of information and their relationships with other "chunks." We call these chunks patterns or frogs. Once frogs are identified they are resolved with ideation and back casting.

Mapping the mess

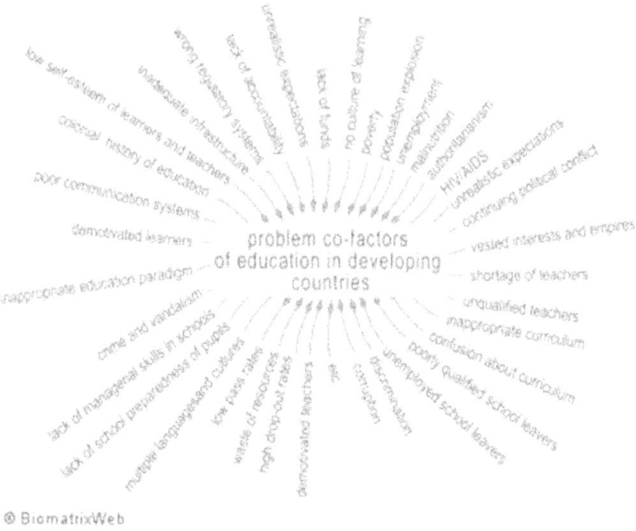
problem co-factors of education in developing countries
demotivated learners
vested interests and empires
shortage of teachers
unqualified teachers
poor communication systems
© BiomatrixWeb

Source: Biomatrix systems theory

Once you understand the mess, you brainstorm the ideal future to dissolve the patterns of the mess and then back cast from the future to the current to create a roadmap of actions.

First, we "kiss the frogs" to create "princes" – what is the ideal situation if we could dissolve this frog effectively?

Finding the frogs

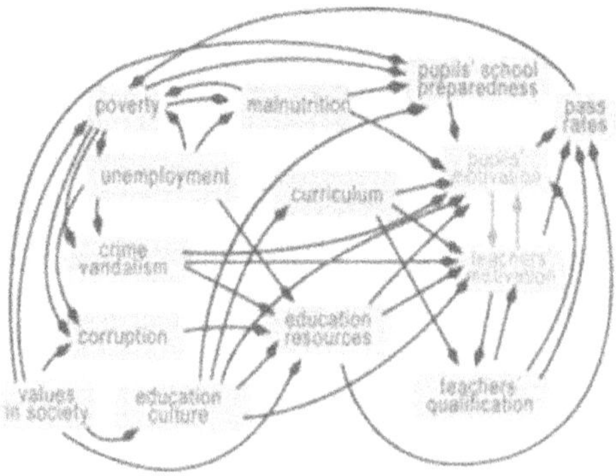
poverty
malnutrition
pupils' school preparedness
pass rates
unemployment
curriculum
crime vandalism
corruption
education resources
values in society
education culture
teachers qualification

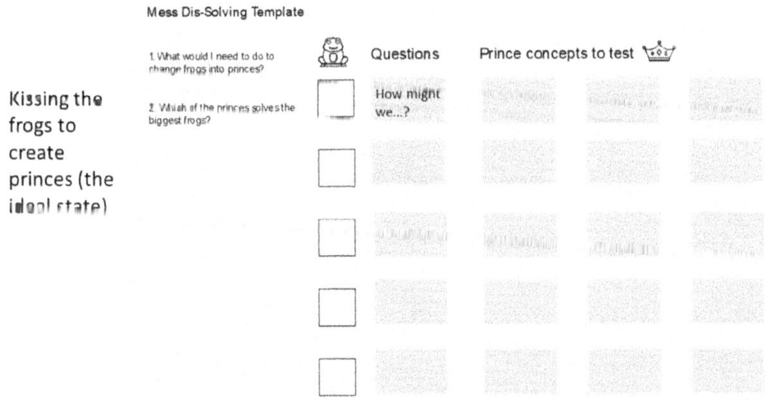
Mess Dis-Solving Template
1. What would I need to do to change frogs into princes?
2. Which of the princes solves the biggest frogs?
Questions
Prince concepts to test
How might we...?
Kissing the frogs to create princes (the ideal state)

Once we clear ideal solutions, we work out everything that we need to be done to get this in place through back casting.

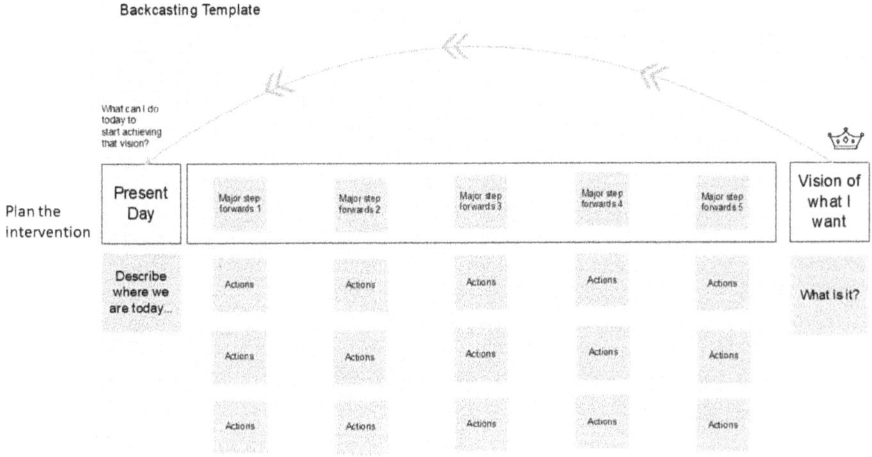
Backcasting Template
What can I do today to start achieving that vision?
Plan the intervention
Present Day
Major step forwards 1
Major step forwards 2
Major step forwards 3
Major step forwards 4
Major step forwards 5
Vision of what I want
Describe where we are today...
Actions
What is it?

Image credit: ARIES

Human Centered Design

Develop Yourself

IDEO Design thinking certificate https://www.ideou.com/products/design-thinking-certificate

Human centred design – introduction – Coursera https://www.coursera.org/learn/human-computer-interaction

Agile Method For Delivery and Performance

Tool

90-day sprints using OKRs: You define the outcomes you'd like to achieve at the end of the next 90 days. It's long enough to give the required "visibility" and align on results to be achieved while being short enough to stay flexible. Stakeholders know what they can expect, and teams know what they are working towards. Everybody is aligned on what needs to be done at the end of the 90 days.

Define your cross-functional projects and outcomes for the next 90 days and write OKRs (objectives and key results) for them. Plan the initiatives and actions to achieve the key results. Measure after 90 days and pivot if required.

90 day sprint

Excellent

Well done

Improvement required

KRA	Objectives	Key result	Period 1	Rating
KRA #1 (LT Strategy) *Rethink the product foundations to meet Enterprise needs*	1.1 *Design a flexible method for customer to categorise and find data*	*Discover the top 3 pain points for enterprise customers through [illegible] the annual feedback survey*	*Interview 10 customers*	EXCELLENT
	1.2			
KRA #2 (Collab measures)	2.1			
	2.2			
KRA#3 (Business Plan – *Significant uplift in sales achieved to remain competitive*	3.1 *Improve our sales performance across the whole team.*	*Maintain a sales pipeline of qualified leads valued at least $500K quarterly.*	*250K achieved*	*IMPROVEMENT REQUIRED*

Storytelling

Questions To Ask

- What stories do people tell about your organisation?
- What reputation is communicated amongst your customers and other stakeholders?
- What do stories say about what your organisation believes in?
- What do employees talk about when they think of the history of the company?
- What stories do they tell new people who join the company?

Where To Start

1. What stood out for me today?
2. Did I hear any good stories?
3. Did I read any good stories?
4. Are there any stories I keep hearing?

For each story you find, ask yourself:

- What is the point this story makes?
- Is it relevant and memorable?

A story describes *what* happened.

A good story helps you *see* what happened.

A great story helps you *feel* what happened.

Courses

Attend an Anecdote program

https://www.anecdote.com/story-programs/

Appendix 2

Chapter 6

Behaviours And Practices

How to do effective sense-making according to Ancona

- Explore the wider system - Seek many types and sources of data. Involve others as you try to make sense of any situation.
- Create a map of the situation - let the proper map or framework emerge from your understanding of the situation. Look for patterns and identify the paradoxes.
- Act to change the system to learn more about it. Ideate to create solutions that could help you respond to the changed system. Learn from experiments and probes.

Seeing around corner practices according to McGrath

- Get out of the building and talk to the future happening now.
- Be willing to listen to disconfirming evidence.
- Have a relentless external focus.
- Articulate a general strategic direction to guide the firm through inflection points.
- Push decision making as close to the edges as possible.

Chapter 7

Behaviours And Practices

Growth Mindset

- Create a new compelling belief: a belief in yourself, your skills and abilities, and your capacity for positive change.
- View failure differently: see failure as an opportunity to learn from your experiences and apply what you have learned next time.
- Hear and interrupt your fixed mindset voice. Recognise that you have a choice. Add "not yet" when you doubt whether you can do something, i.e., I am not good at this…yet OR replace "I am not good at this" with "I am just getting started".
- Be curious and commit to lifelong learning: try to adopt the attitude of a child, looking at the world around you with awe and wonderment; ask questions and truly listen to the answers.
- Do what is uncomfortable and challenging – that is where the learning is.
- Instead of overfocusing on the problem, ask what can be done to solve it. Act and learn.
- Reflect often: "Describe a time you confronted a challenge. How did you work through it to overcome your doubts?"

Curiosity

Applying a little structure to your curiosity helps you act. It looks like this:

Start with a question about something you're curious about.

Now ask several sub-questions related to that first question. For each answer you identify…

- See if there are further sub-questions to ask.
- Answer each of those to your satisfaction.
- Then collate your answers up to a level.
- And finally, come back to answer your first question.
- Now what can you do with your answer? What's an action you can take?
- Or is there a new question you want to ask?

https://www.curiosityjournals.com/blogs/news/why-curiosity-is-the-actual-secret-behind-the-growth-mindset

Self-Awareness

Behaviours And Practices

Self-management is a conscious choice to resist a preference or habit and instead, show a more productive behaviour. It's a four-step process:

1. **Be present.** Pay attention to what is happening in this moment — not what was said 15 minutes ago or what will happen in your next meeting.
2. **Be self-aware.** What are you seeing, hearing, feeling, doing, saying, and considering?
3. **Identify a range of behavioural choices.** What do you want to do next? What are the possible consequences of each action? What feedback have you gotten that might inform your choices?

What are some alternative choices you can make — even if they're not what you want to do or what you usually do?

4. **Intentionally choose behaviours believed to be the most productive.** What behaviour will generate the best outcome—even if it's not the behaviour that comes easiest to you?

Porter, HBR

Grit

Behaviours And Practices

1. Find and pursue your passions – we direct more effort to things we are passionate about.
2. Be deliberate about what you focus on and give attention to.
3. Take risks to push yourself out of your comfort zone and stick with it.
4. Seek meaning in what you do.
5. Prioritisation is key.
6. Be more patient.
7. Know when not to grit – is this the right goal for you to continue pursuing? Is this job still right for me?

Emotional Agility

Behaviours And Practices

- Emotionally agile leaders understand they set the tone for what is appropriate regarding emotional expression in their organizations.

- Emotionally agile leaders express a broad range of emotions in ways and in doing so, let their workers do the same.
- Emotionally agile leaders provide their workers' outlets for emotional expression and acknowledge the importance of venting out hard feelings, that will otherwise translate into gossiping, backstabbing, and complaining.
- Emotionally agile leaders are empathic, which enables them to understand that relentless positivity is not the only way to get positive, and constructive results.
- Emotionally agile leaders are curious and compassionate towards their workers' personal experiences.
- Emotionally agile leaders ultimately realize that their success depends on their ability to choose the healthy and appropriate emotional response to a situation.

Focus and Deep Work

Behaviours And Practices

You are the master of your calendar, not the other way around. You put things in your calendar to help you do the right things. But if your needs change, that's OK, change your calendar! Also, lessen your distractions. Starting your day with a plan is the best way to approach deep work. While it's important to acknowledge a day typically won't go exactly as planned, it's important to set a strategy regardless.

But stay focused. If we keep switching tasks, we have what Leroy calls attention residue and perform poorer on the next task. The more intense the residue, the worse the performance. Every time you glance at your emails, you create attention residue. Spend enough time in a state of frenetic shallowness, and you permanently reduce your capacity for deep work.

Chapter 8

Behaviours And Practices

Ethical leadership encompasses many things but ultimately boils down to these six main elements.

1. **Honesty.** Honesty makes ethical leaders worthy of the trust others place in them. It means leaders commit to presenting facts as they are, playing fair with competitors, and communicating honestly with others.
2. **Justice.** To be fair means to treat everyone equally, offer opportunities with no favouritism, and condemn improper behaviours and manipulations, as well as any other actions that could harm someone.
3. **Respect.** Ethical leaders respect others around them, despite their position or identifying features. This means they listen to each stakeholder, foster inclusion, and value diversity.
4. **Integrity.** Integrity is shown when values, words, and actions are aligned and consistent. It is not enough to talk the talk; one must walk the walk to show integrity.
5. **Responsibility.** Responsibility means accepting to be in charge, embracing the power and duties that come with it, and always responding and being present in challenging situations.
6. **Transparency.** Transparency mainly concerns communication with all stakeholders. It means keeping an open dialogue,

accepting feedback, and disclosing the information others need to deliver their work.

https://www.betterup.com/blog/the-importance-of-an-ethical-leader

Chapter 9

Behaviours And Practices

Rooke suggests six key transforming-type capabilities that are worth being nurtured, whether you're profiled as an expert, an achiever, or a redefining type:

1) **Inquiry-based experimentation**

Leaders should have the capacity to adopt an inquiring approach. They must be willing to ask questions and experiment to do things differently.

2) **Sliding between the big picture and small details**

Leaders should be able to seamlessly transition from paying attention to little details to looking at the big picture. Pay attention to both the vision and the details because, according to Rooke, these small details form the vision.

3) **Courageous use of power**

A transformational leader has the courage to tell the truth to authority.

4) **Positive use of language**

Transformational leaders can bring positivity to their brand of leadership, enabling them to appreciate what's working while remaining critical of what's ineffective. This is key to starting the process of transforming your organisation.

5) Taking systems perspective and leadership

This requires you to essentially act into the system and prepares you to become a systems leader and to take on everything that comes with it.

6) Passionate detachment

Be passionate, but you should also be able to cultivate the ability to be detached. This gives you balance and the ability to be more objective.

https://awarego.org/stages-of-transformational-leadership-development/

Chapter 10

Behaviours And Practices

1. Make information available.
2. Organise cross silo dialogues.
3. Urge everyone to build new relationships and networks.
4. Listen to and encourage diverse perspectives.
5. Set collaboration as a goal and measure it.
6. Understand how collaboration works in a hybrid environment – co-create with the team.
7. Invest in collaboration tools.
8. Be clear about who makes the decision in the end.

www.ingramcontent.com/pod-product-compliance
Lightning Source LLC
Chambersburg PA
CBHW040920210326
41597CB00030B/5141
9781915502575